Beneath The Elm Tree

Betty Lankers

*For everything there is a
season, and a time for every
mattter under heaven...*

Ecclesiastes 3:1

Beneath The Elm Tree

East View Farm Vignettes from the 1940's & 1950's

By Betty Palmquist Lankers

The Old Granary Publishing
2014

First Printing: 2012

ISBN 978-1-304-82096-9

The Old Granary Publishing
Bristol, IL 60512

theoldgranaryevf@gmail.com

Beneath the Elm Tree

A giant elm tree guarded the gateway to East View Farm,
With thick, dark green boughs bent wide and free.
It's chestnut brown trunk stood broad, sturdy, and strong,
With a heavy canopy of leaves that shaded the hidden nests.
A giant elm tree guarded the gateway to East View Farm.

Underneath this spreading elm
A family lived long and alive
Days rich with activities
Nights calm with restful sleep
Underneath this spreading elm

Now all but memories remain of the elm and life so long ago.
Past events march into history,
The ancient elm into new soil and air,
Paving the way for new trees and new people and new happenings
Part of life's cycle of endings leading to new beginnings.
Now all but memories remain of the elm and life so long ago.

Betty Lankers

Vignettes

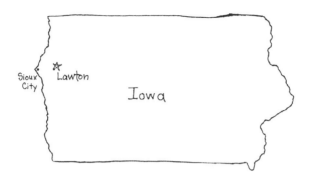

BEFORE WORDS

Historian Dorothy Schwieder has written, "If the Midwest is the nation's heartland, then perhaps Iowa is the heart itself, pulsating quietly, slowly, and evenly, blending together the physical and social features of the entire region." Ron Fisher includes the above descriptive quotation in his book, Heartland of a Continent. He continues his own physical explanations of Iowa. Ron writes, "Iowa is the heart of the Midwestern breadbasket, where the world's most successful agriculture is practiced. The breadbasket produces one third of the world's soybeans, three-fourths of the continent's wheat and corn, and many of its cattle and pigs. The land is amazingly fertile. The topsoil here may be seven feet deep, and some of the grasses grow roots half an inch thick."

Iowa is the place where I was born and raised. My older sister Charlotte, my younger brother Carl and I grew up on a farm in the northwestern tip of Iowa near where South Dakota and Nebraska meet at the Missouri River in Sioux City, Iowa. We lived on East View Farm, which was near Lawton, Iowa, a little town about ten miles east of Sioux City. Not only do the roots of the grasses in this area grow thick and stretch extensively in the rich soils of Iowa but memories of life there also extend sustained and precious, lingering in the hearts of those of us who were privileged to grow into adulthood there.

This writing started for me with a short fun excursion into my past; a simple writing exercise. I started thinking about Mom's cook stove. The more I wrote, the more fun I had. Other topics came to mind and away I went. The memories written were for my girls, Lisa and Katie, to understand how their Mom grew up in a different time, place, and culture. I think I was exploring who I was and how my development was formed by my place of birth, family, and life some seventy years ago.

In the midst of the collecting of materials for the vignettes a recipe for making soap was found and it circulated in our family. A young Benjamin Lewis, a great-nephew in Colorado read the recipe and exclaimed, "You mean they MADE soap?!" Now I was sure my mission in writing a nearly forgotten way of life was valid.

Charlotte was consulted often and made many great suggestions. Carl added technical details, brand particulars and operations of household appliances, especially to the farming section with pertinent names and specific ideas. Lisa was instrumental in the scanning, inserting, designing and formatting these vignettes into a book.

I know there are probably still errors in my tales and anecdotes but I have tried to be as accurate as possible when writing. In remembering events and happenings in the 1940's and 1950's it all came to life again in words and ideas. It is an existence long passed by in our modern world but real in my memories. Deep in our souls lay the foundation of who we are today.

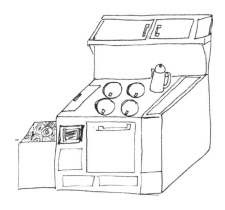

Mom's Cook Stove

Nothing works as hard in any kitchen today as the cook stove of yesterday. At least in the Palmquist household it did. In one unified piece of mechanical genius, the cook stove took a central place in the East View Farm kitchen as an appliance which served many functions. The brand name of Mom's prize white metal cook stove was Renown, but the cook stove's name does not begin to tell us anything about the importance of this piece of equipment in the early days of the East View kitchen.

The most basic task of the cook stove, of course, was preparation of food for our busy family. Beside the cook stove in Mom's kitchen stood a propane fueled gas stove, but in the early days the cook stove was the work-horse when it came to making meals and keeping warm water available.

Before one could even think of starting the fire in the firebox of the stove, the cob box needed to be filled and some firewood in a wooden box would be stashed nearby to add to the fire once the flames began. This was a job to be completed each evening. Cobs were stored down in the cob room in the northeast corner of the basement. These came in ready supply at East View. Every summer a large machine called a sheller came to separate the golden corn from the rough cobs. The corn crib was emptied of the previous year's crop and after the removal of the kernels of corn by the giant sheller, a supply of the red cobs was always handy. A whole wagon load was brought into the house through a small north basement window to fill the cob bin along with a mouse or two. Cats generally took care of the mouse problem so it was just a matter of carrying the cobs upstairs to get the fire started. The cats did provide another problem though as they seemed to think the cob bin could be a giant litter box, although their preferred place of deposit was the sand surface on the top of the furnace in the basement. When the weather got cold and they were privileged to come in to warm up, they left unwelcome calling cards.

Fires in the cook stove started easily using giant wooden or farmer matches. They were stored in a rectangular match holder on the wall of the chimney nearby. Easy starting materials were placed in the firebox on the left side of the cook stove and ignition promised good things to come. Cobs used to light the first fire of the day were often dipped in kerosene which was stored in a can on the shelf over the basement stairs. The ignition came quickly and soon longer burning chopped wood pieces were inserted.

Once the fire warmed the black iron stovetop, cooking could proceed. If just one pan was needed, to cook oatmeal for example, heat was needed only under one part of the top. Several circles on the stovetop could be lifted with a tool much like a giant key inserted in a lock. The circles lifted so burning material could be moved underneath and thus control the amount of warmth radiating into the bubbling pan above. Waxed material from Wonder and Old Home bread wrappers was rubbed over the hot range to polish the black iron of the stove top to a satin patina.

Biscuits, bread, cookies, and cake would need the oven located in the lower center of the cook stove much like ovens in kitchens today. Now, not just the top would need heating but the whole oven. Careful use of the burning materials was a must to achieve correct temperatures.

For this reason most of Mom's baking was done in the propane oven. Mom always used the propane stove for the more intricate specialties like cakes, especially angel food cake. A small propane tank for the stove's use was located just west of the house. So as to conserve on the use of propane, a day was set aside just for that oven's use each week. Thursdays were baking days. Usually with the gas oven on and hot, it was used over and over for favorites like Swedish braided coffee cakes and rye bread, then perhaps some cookies, and often a cake like Mom's favorite throw-together chocolate cake or hot milk cake but never just one thing as that would be a wasteful squandering of heat once the oven was hot.

One of Mom's specialties which made it to the table first was flat bread from the Swedish rye recipe. Regular loaves were made and extra dough was formed into a round, smooth bread which often was served to us warm when we came home from school or at the latest, supper time. I don't know which was better, the taste of the fennel and anise flavored bread or the aroma of the spices and rye flour baking. Last in the oven was a recipe Mom used often. It was called Forgotten Desert. This was a meringue mixture flattened on a cake pan. She put it in the oven at the end of baking time, turned off the oven and let the heat of the oven bake it to a crisp light finish. She often served this specialty on Sundays with strawberries or other fruit on top with a dollop of fresh farm whipped cream.

On the right side of the cook stove, beside the oven, was the water reservoir. It was a copper tank which was always filled to the brim with warm water just waiting for a dipper to plunge in and make use of the already tepid water to start the potatoes cooking, supply water for soaking dishes or heating for baths or any of the thousand uses our hot water heaters have today. A tea kettle often sat closer to the center of the fires, ready for any need of water at higher temperatures like doing dishes or preparing Jell-O.

Just to the left of the vat for the water was the perfect place for the coffee pot to sit to keep warm. At breakfast the coffee bubbled on the hot left grid, promising a tasty brew to accompany the morning pancakes or cereal. Then the pot was moved to the right side of the stove to silently wait for mail time at 10:00. Then, curious readers gathered and sipped their second cup while reading the day's mail and newspaper. The same usefulness occurred with the noon coffee. It was kept warm or another pot prepared for the afternoon coffee time at 3:30 or so. A piece of cake, cookie, or perhaps a rusk made from homemade dinner rolls sliced and toasted with a cinnamon-

sugar topping or some kind of treat always accompanied this cup of coffee. Sometimes Mom topped soda crackers with cheese which she melted in the oven if it was being used that afternoon. When Mom made fruit pies, leftover over pieces of pie dough were baked alongside and were especially prized treats. Much work was yet to be done on the farm before supper so calories were not even considered. There were cows to be brought in from the pasture and milked, calves, chickens, and perhaps some pigs to feed and all the chores it takes every evening to make the day complete.

Above the stove were smaller metal doors which when opened could be used as warming areas for rolls. As supper was cooking, they were handy areas for keeping salt and pepper to add to the dishes to be served or as a place to store hot pads. When dish towels were hung over the top, the cook stove became a dryer. During the winter months assortments of mittens and other damp clothes found their way close to the stove to dry and get ready for the next escapade outside.

Mom's cook stove stood on the east wall of her kitchen. Not only was it the first thing seen when coming downstairs, it's warmth was a pleasant contrast from the cold upstairs. During the night, the huge coal and wood-burning furnace down in the basement would lose its fire power and until the new flames of the day could take over, a chill pervaded the house. Dressing for school in the mornings was as quick an affair as possible. In the kitchen the warmth of the fire burning in the cookstove provided a cozy snug welcome not only in the early dark winter mornings but also in the evenings when our family gathered near the stove to eat our supper after the day's work and chores were completed. The people sitting with their backs to the stove enjoyed extra comfort compared to the people near the outside white brick finished wall to the west where the wintry wind often blew from the cottonwoods on the nearby hill at the edge of the orchard.

Part of the warm ambiance of the cook stove came from the heat emanating from the black tin pipes which connected the stove to the nearby chimney. Every spring a day came when it was a must to clean out the pipes. Newspapers were laid everywhere to catch the soot when the sections were separated. This was always a very hazardous dirty job if not done carefully. Cecil Hilman, an Earl May seed salesman, seemed to always hit this day selling seed corn for spring planting to Dad. One day another man came to visit the family. He stopped to help when he saw what was going on and ended up on a ladder holding a pipe. Suddenly his pants began to fall! He managed to hold them up with one hand with his other arm around the black sooty pipe. How Mom and Aunt Ruth loved to tell this story!! I remember the day well. It was either Mom's Uncle Luther Anderson or a Swedish neighbor from Bronson and fellow Augustana church member, Oscar Peterson, who held the pipe and pants so precariously on that ladder. I was very young and I remember whoever held the pipe was a very large man. My Mom and Aunt Ruth were helped through the rest of their lives by the humor of that day along with the aid he provided in removal of the soot. Farm kitchens could always use a helping hand.

The cook stove helped in another way other than cooking and baking. It heated irons used for pressing washed wrinkled items. Before East View Farm electronically came of age and was wired to the Rural Electric Cooperative (the REA) system in 1947, the cook stove heated six inch long elliptical slabs of iron which fit into a waiting metal hood. These pieces of iron were flat on the top and bottom. After heating the iron pieces on the top of the cook stove they were secured in the waiting metal hood. On top was a wooden round handle which enabled the person using it to iron clothes, sheets, pillow cases, tablecloths, dishcloths and any other pieces of wash which seemed necessary to press into smooth submission. A waxy surface like a bread wrapper or waxed paper was often used to rub over the bottom of the iron before it touched the clothes. This kept the iron from sticking to the fabrics, cleaned it, and made the ironing motions smooth. No fabrics in those days were easy-care. All needed at least a quick pressing to look presentable except Dad's overalls of course and other old clothes used for outside work.

During the summer months when the cook stove was not working diligently all day with the soups, stews, Dutch ovens with roasts, coffee, and baking, a fuel fed iron was used so heat from the stove was not demanded. Mom lit the flame to heat this blue-green iron with white-gas held in a silver round container on the side of this more modern pressing agent of its day. Air was pumped into the fuel and a match was used to ignite the fire which created the heat. The iron itself looked much like the irons of today but was heated by fire directly in the iron itself.

When natural gas was eventually piped into the house in 1956 from the main Texas to Minnesota line which ran through the bottom land east of the farm buildings, Mom got a modern gas stove. The low cost, ease, speed, and control of turning on the burners and oven of this advanced appliance made the old propane and cook stove seem like an antique old-fashioned way to prepare food. Now the cook stove became a place to store food. Mom hid cookies she made in the back of the oven in tins to keep them safe from many hungry fingers and filled the rest of the oven and areas above with boxes of dry food like crackers, cereal or popcorn ready to pop.

The cook stove days were a time when life moved at a slower pace. There was always time for stories and sharing, for evening devotions after supper as a family, reading events in the newspaper, and talking near-by the stove with visiting neighbors, family, and friends. Today our modern stoves along with our microwave ovens provide immediate heat and make available instantaneous meals with our instant potatoes, minute rice, canned and dried soups and the myriad of other foods we can immediately put on our tables in a twinkling of an eye. Somehow in all our rush to make our lives easier something has been lost. Cook stoves provided physical warmth but when I look back to evenings in the kitchen playing Flinch, Old Maid, Rook or some favorite board game we always were in the kitchen in front of the cook stove. We often made fudge, or divinity. I even remember pulling taffy one wintry Sunday afternoon. Dad's favorite activity was popping corn in the old black manually turned pan he dug out of an upper cupboard over the back door.

It seems the cook stove in the kitchen had work beyond its cooking and baking capabilities. The legacy of the cook stove extended far beyond temperature but radiated the ambiance of family activities together, hospitality for guests and a warm generosity of days long gone. At least at East View Farm this was true.

Swedish Rye Bread

1 qt lukewarm water
4 tbsp shortening (melted)
2 heaping tsp salt
¼ cup white sugar
1 cup brown sugar
2 tbsp molasses
1 1/2 tsp crushed fennel
1 1/2 tsp crushed anise

Put all ingredients in the lukewarm water. Add 4 cups rye flour and 2 cakes of dissolved yeast. (Dissolve yeast in a little lukewarm water). Stir all together, make batter stiff by adding from about 8 to 10 cups of white flour. Let rise until double in size, work down, and let rise again. Then make into loaves. Let loaves raise until double in size.

Bake in moderate oven for about 1 hour.

Hannah Swanson
from the Augustana Miriam Cookbook

Forgotten Dessert

5 egg whites
1 ½ cups sugar
Pinch of salt and ½ tsp cream of tartar

Heat oven to 400 degrees. Turn oven off when putting in dessert and leave it in the oven overnight. It will keep in refrigerator several days.

Top with strawberries and whipped cream or ice cream.

Hot Milk Cake

4 eggs
2 cups sugar
2 cups flour
2 tsp baking powder
1 cup milk
½ cup butter

Beat eggs, add sugar and beat until it bubbles. Add flour, mixed and sifted with baking powder and beat again. Melt butter in milk and pour all in. Have milk almost boiling hot, but do not boil. Can also add nuts. Bake in a 350 degree oven 30-35 minutes.

Topping:
2/3 cup brown sugar
4 tbsp cream
1 cup coconut flakes
4 tsp melted butter
2 tsp vanilla

Combine and spread on top of cake. Put under broiler a few minutes until golden. Watch carefully.

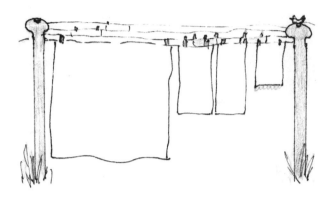

WARsh Day

Every Monday dawned too soon at East View. This was the washing day. All too early the sun rose this day and the task of cleaning last week's dirtiness must begin. Even the food on this day took on regular simplicity. Often it was a casserole called Roman Holiday, a mixture of browned loose hamburger, elbow macaroni, canned tomatoes, a liberal sprinkling of pepper, salt, onion, and cheese. Both Aunt Ruth and Mom spent the day with the duties of getting all dirty fabric clean. This had to be done each Monday.

Washing took lots of preparation. Not only must all the clothes, linens, and towels be collected from all floors of the house, but all socks must be accounted for no matter how many trips up and down the stairs one must make. Water for the washer was heated in a tall, oval, copper container on a small, black stove by the chimney in the basement. This was set up on Sunday evening with starting material and wood ready to light the fire on Monday morning. All the water did not need to be hot. The two rinses were simply cold water drawn in pails and carried to the rinsing tubs.

After the assortment of soiled materials collected from the house came basketed to the basement, the next task was to attempt to sort them into piles following a continuum from fine whites, bed linens, good clothes, everyday clothes, towels, and finally the pile of the very dirty and sometimes grease covered work overalls and rags. This was super important as only one load of water in the wringer machine was used for ALL the washing. The first loads were the fortunate ones.

Before electricity came to East View Farm in 1947, a wooden washing machine was used which was powered by a Willy's Valve silent sleeve engine. Electricity was created by wind through the blades of a Wincharger set high on a metal tower on the hill outside west of the house. This powered a Delco 32 volt light plant which was used to create electricity for East View Farm. This electricity was stored in heavy, tall glass battery containers in the basement. Wind was essential. No wind, no wash. The barrel stave constructed washer swished and agitated the clothes around and back and forth to clean them and they were wrung out with the wringer.

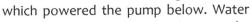

Electricity was not the only wind powered gift. The very water used for everything at East View Farm came from a windmill located on a high hill south of the farm buildings. Large blades of the tall windmill caught the wind which powered the pump below. Water was pumped into a cement cistern and a buried pipe took the water down the long hill south of the house to provide all the water needed for the house and barn. Enough pressure was created by the downhill journey so it could be used in the second floor bathroom of the house. Dad had a ladder which went down into the holding area so it could be cleaned. A long wooden rod was secured on the tall metal tower which held the pumping mechanism and wind blades. Dad took the rod down to measure and find the depth of the water in the reservoir so the windmill could be turned on when necessary and turned off when full.

This chore was often a leisurely Sunday evening adventure for us kids with Dad. These trips to check the water level were important for at no time should the tank become low as then the possibility of no water existed if the breezes were not found. No wind, no water, NO GOOD! The harnessed winds from the western prairie made life easier for all.

Water was the main ingredient for washing, but this very water which cleaned must be removed before the drying could take place. After the clothes came out of the washer, this was done with the wringer. The wringer arrangement which best suited the rinsing tubs and washing machine was in a square. The wringer on the washing machine consisted of two white horizontal, rubberized circular columns which rolled round and round inside a metal casing. They pressed out the excess water and moved the clean material to the next rinsing stage.

Sometimes in the very hot first wash loads a round, wooden stick had to be used to get the individual garments out of the very sudsy hot water to put in the wringer. The first rinse tub sat directly beside the washer. The wringer then swung around to wring out the objects after they had been rinsed up and down in the first water. This first rinse took most of the soap out. The second water had some bluing liquid put into the water to help  the whites glisten with cleanliness. The bars of the wringer then took the last bit of moisture out before the clean washed garments and household things went into a round, wooden, fabric lined bushel basket, ready to take up the stairs and outside to hang on the lines south of the house. Sometimes there were problems. Fingers could easily get caught in the rolling wringers so there was a snap to release the rollers to free the caught hand. After squeezing the moisture from one load the wringer was readied again over the washing machine to proceed with the next load. One batch of wash was always agitating while the previous load was rinsing and hung out on the lines to dry in the fresh air.

The first lucky load was always the finest tablecloths used during the week or fancy lingerie and such. The next load was the white sheets. Sheets were always white and they must stay WHITE. The bright, newly washed sheets hung at the far eastern end of the clotheslines, always the first things out. Underwear was always hung on the back lines to make sure no one passing on the road, the milkman, postman, visiting guests, and/or salesmen could see them. There were uncompromisable rules enforced with zeal for hanging out the wash and this was not just at East View. There is a modern remembering of these rules which was sent to me by an e-mail which recalls the code for drying clothes. It is as follows:

RULES FOR CLOTHESLINES

1. You had to wash the clothes line before hanging any clothes by walking the entire lengths of each line with a damp cloth around the lines.

2. You had to hang the clothes in a certain order and always hang "whites" with "whites" and hang them first.

3. You never hung a shirt by the shoulders but always by the tail! What would neighbors think? Clothes pins were always placed on side seams.

4. Wash day is on a Monday! Never hang clothes on the weekend or Sunday for Heaven's sake!

5. Hang the sheets and towels on the outside lines so you could hide your "unmentionables" in the middle. (perverts and busybodies, y'know!)

6. It did not matter if it was sub zero weather. Clothes would "freeze-dry".

7. Always gather the clothes pins when taking down dry clothes! Pins left on the lines were "tacky"!

8. If you were efficient, you would line the clothes up so that each item did not need two clothes pins, but shared one of the clothes pins with the next washed item. This worked especially well for towels and other flat items.

9. Clothes must be off of the line before dinner time, neatly folded in the clothes basket and ready to be ironed.

10. IRONED?! Well, that's a whole other subject!

At East View this whole washing and drying operation took all of Monday. After the whites were finished, the rest of the loads came next, separated according to color and dirtiness. The last loads of very dirty work clothes swished in gray water and by the time they came out, looked amazingly dirt free, not a bit like the dark, muddy water they came out of. Miracle of miracles, all fabrics were clean when the day was done.

Alongside the square arrangement of washing machine, rinsing tubs and carryout baskets there was always a tub with some soapy water and a washboard. This was used to pre-clean stubborn spots. Using a square of strong handmade soap, the fabric was scrubbed hard by hand up and down the corrugated metal to get rid of the stain. One of Mom's favorite soaps was one she made herself with suet drippings, lye and other agents. She cooked the mixture and it was poured into white tea towel lined wooden peach boxes. When the boiled mixture finished drying or curing, the soap was cut into small rectangles or bars. Dirt had no chance with Mom's specially made dirt chasers.

Another special process had to be prepared on East View wash days. It was started early on the wash day. Water was heated on the kitchen stove separately from the water heated for the washing machine in the basement. This water was poured into an oval white dishpan and was used to make a starching solution for some of the washing. Argo Corn Starch from a blue box (to show the difference to regular corn starch for cooking in a yellow box) was used along with squares of a blue waxy agent which Mom broke from a Hershey-like bar. This made the pressing much smoother when ironing the starched clothes and the smell was what is known today as "clean linen" in sachets in the modern 2000's world. Fabrics which needed a little extra body were put in the starch liquid and wrung out after the last rinse. Examples of objects needing starch might be the everyday hardworking aprons and cotton print housedresses for extra protection from stains and wear, white shirt collars and cuffs for body, and sometimes objects like dresser scarves and crocheted doilies were starched just for their smooth appearance when they were ironed.

During the winter when putting the clothes out on the line was an impossible task because of blizzards or excess below zero cold, they were hung on lines in the basement of the house. The saturated garments added humidity to our home as they dried which was part of the reason lines were put there in the first place. When possible, the wash was hung outside and came into the house frozen, dry, and stiff; smelling of fresh promised new snow.

Each year when winter had passed, a pair of wrens always arrived each spring to set up their housekeeping in the top of the west clothes pole. Most days the cheerful calls of the busy feathered residents provided happy spring and summer background sounds to whatever was happening in the kitchen or nearby. On Mondays the wren's territory was invaded by the serious activity of washing and drying clothes and the tiny wrens protested loudly. The scolding which went on each Monday only added to the annoyance of the day for the washer women but provoked wry smiles on their faces as they continued their wash hanging amidst the chagrin of the wrens intent on protecting their home. The advent of fall at East View was always

anticipated by the migration time of the wrens. When they left it was a sign that the first frost was to arrive six weeks later.

Bird battles continued on all sides of the clotheslines. On the west side it was the wrens and from the east side of the lines other birds bombarded the washing process with unwanted droppings. In the summer when the mulberry tree growing directly east of the clotheslines provided the local birds with food, the resulting stain plopped on the newly washed sheets and other carefully cleaned items when the birds flew off provided a very provoking situation for Mom. With the discolored item in her hand she quickly bustled over to the outside faucet to try and get the dark, purple splotch out as soon as possible with a sputtering of anger. After the rinsing, the washing process had to start again for each stained item, only this time by hand. Not a good thing on a Monday washday.

When the loads of wash were finally clean, the water from all the washing and rinsing was then carried out in five gallon pails to be poured outside. Before putting everything away, the basement was scrubbed with a mop which was made with rags secured by a six to eight inch metal clip. Wringing out this mop was done by hand. The wash water not only scrubbed the basement floor but the stairs going down to the basement and the landing and stairs just inside the back door were scoured. Then newspapers were put down in an attempt to catch the first couple day's muddy materials drug in from outside.

Late on Monday afternoons, "warshing" day was finally done. Coffee time brought welcome relaxation. Clothes and sheets lay around the dining room, brought in from outside with a fresh smell not to be duplicated by any of the finest potpourris or room sprays. The clean piles waited to be put away or to be ironed, but that story belongs to Tuesday, ironing day.

Roman Holiday

1 lb hamburger
1 tsp salt
1/8 tsp pepper
1 onion
¼ cup Crisco
1 ½ cups canned tomatoes
2 cups chopped spaghetti cooked (Mom always used elbow macaroni)
¾ cup grated cheese

Fry onion in Crisco, add meat and seasonings. Cook 5 minutes. Make layer of spaghetti in baking dish, add meat mixture and its drippings. Then add another layer of spaghetti. Pour in tomatoes, sprinkle with grated cheese, cover dish, and bake in moderate oven 35 minutes. Remove cover, bake 10 minutes longer. (Mushrooms can be added if desired).

Hannah Swanson
from the Augustana Miriam Cookbook

Laundry Soap

5 lbs cracklings or old lard
6 qts water
1 can lye
1 cup bleach **OR** 1 cup ammonia as preferred

Stir for 5 days and the 6th day cook – and put into boxes to set.

Lorraine Hess

Please note: This recipe mentions using bleach and it also mentions ammonia. They were alternative cleaning agents to choose from to add to the soap. They should **NEVER, NEVER** be used together or poisonous gases will form which are deadly.

This soap was in a thick liquid form when cooked and was poured into wooden peach boxes lined with white dish towels to harden in the cool basement. Then squares of the soap were cut with a sharp knife and were used in the laundry to remove stains and hard to remove dirt from items.

East View Farm Produce Market

Flowers at East View Farm consisted of some ever-growing, seemingly perpetual lavender petunias self-seeded annually on the northeast side of the house and a coral bell plant which bloomed directly in front of the house. A sweetly scented mock orange bush grew near the clothesline and some pink wild rose bushes punctuated the hillside behind the house. Shrubs filled the foundation plantings to the front of the house.

But the real gardening at East View could be found in the vegetable gardens. Each year three places were secured and set aside from the regular grain production to be used for growing our family's food which would be used all year. There were also two other permanent gardening spaces; a fenced in garden on a knoll just south of the house and in an orchard of the farm across the road. In another orchard to the west of East View's buildings there was an immense apple tree below the towering cottonwoods at the top of the hill. A crab apple tree along with some wild plums surrounded the brooder house west of the house.

One small area of the farm was set aside each spring for growing potatoes. Potatoes were stored in a cave near the house. Since the cave provided great year around protection for the potatoes, potatoes from the last year were used to produce the new crop. Eyes, or places on the potato built for reproduction, were carefully cut dividing each potato into many new plant starters. A new plant would be replicated with each eye-section cut with the paring knife. These were planted in early spring in rows Dad plowed with his Ford tractor and planter to make the furrows. Behind, in the soil, we would place the cut white pieces of potato in the dark soil. They were covered and Mother Nature did her production work all summer.

Sometimes potato beetles were found in the patch as the plants matured and it was a task to walk among the plants with small containers and remove them manually as much as possible. When one is a gardener one has to watch and tend the plants carefully all season for not only weeds but pests.

In the fall, after the potato plants had died down, when their growing work underground was done, our family would take a Saturday and dig them. Once again, Dad would use an implement to plow them and throw the new "spuds" on top of the soil. I remember one particular Saturday when the potato patch was located north of the pasture near the swamp area. The potatoes piled high everywhere on top of the newly turned black soil.

potatoes

Mom and Dad looked at this giant task of harvesting and decided to set a goal. They made a promise: if all the potatoes were in the cave by the end of the day, our whole family would go out to eat after church on Sunday. NOW this was UNHEARD of! All of us OUT TO EAT?! And Mom admitted later, they never thought it would be possible for all of the potatoes to be harvested in that one day.

BUT, three children had a glimpse of a dream and the potatoes were gathered with intensity. By nightfall the potatoes were collected in a huge pile in the northwest corner of the cave. The next day our family went out to dinner! We went to a restaurant on a Sioux City corner called the Arcadia where a cousin, Agnes Haglund worked. It was a great meal with white linen cloths and napkins, special not only with the tastes of the food but the feeling of satisfaction as a family of a task completed and celebrated.

Dad often left some space along his corn fields somewhere to plant sweet corn and sporadically when we needed it he planted popcorn. The sweet corn was often planted directly across the road from the buildings so the ripening process could be monitored. We were not the only ones watching the maturing of the golden grains. The local raccoons seemed to uncannily know when the picking time was ready and they took great advantage of our crops if possible. Both Mom and Dad and the raccoons must have carefully checked the cobs regularly. The raccoons would slip the husks down just a little bit much as we did and wait until the perfect ripened moment. I remember listening to them one warm moonlit early August night as they began their attack on

corn

the stalks in a patch just across the road from our buildings. Mom and Dad heard them too and we all went out with kerosene lanterns which we left dangling on poles in the field the rest of the night. Raccoons do not like light so the corn was safe that year. If the corn patch was farther away we were not always so lucky.

When the sweet corn was picked in the early days it was canned along with the other vegetables. After the freezer was purchased, corn was frozen in large amounts as it was easy to handle and so good to cook buttered in the winter or make corn pudding. The cobs of corn were blanched and cooled. Then the corn kernels were cut was off by sharp knives and frozen.

The main kitchen garden which supplied the rest of the vegetables our family ate was always located close to the house so we could tend it easily. Often it was right across the road or just south of the buildings. One of the major plants grown was the tomatoes. Mom always insisted on buying 50 or so "field grown" tomato plants. We would go in to Earl May Seed and Feed downtown in Sioux City and go to a back room where they had large pails with water. In the water were plants tied in bundles of twenty-five. No soil, just well-rooted plants. We took them home, planted them deeply, and every year we had a bountiful tomato crop. Besides eating our fill of fresh tomatoes, tomatoes were canned. We canned cut up tomatoes to add to chili, make tomato and other soups, Swiss steak and many foods which called for them. We canned tomato juice which we used in the mornings like orange juice. Rows of the red jars lined shelves for use all winter. Other plants Mom bought to add to the garden were cabbage for making slaw in the summer and stuffed cabbage rolls and green peppers for salads and cooking.

The fruit room, as we called a small especially built room in the basement, was filled to capacity by each October. Grandpa Johnson built the fruit room for Mom just for this purpose. Wooden shelves lined all walls of this rectangular area and they were filled with not only tomato produce but fruits the orchards yielded like apple sauce, apple juice, apple jelly, and crab apple pickles, along with plum and cherry sauces. By the end of harvest, pickles of many varieties had been carefully made with vinegars and fragrant spices. There were cucumber pickles of all types like dill, sweet, crisp sliced sandwich pickles, ripe cucumber pickles, and bread and butter pickles. Each season, at least one batch of watermelon pickles was made from the rind of this favorite summer fruit. Nothing was wasted in the East View kitchen. All was used.

Each August Mom looked forward to the shipments of Colorado peaches which she canned. They came to grocery stores in about twenty pound wooden lugs. Pears were another fruit she purchased to prepare for winter meals. She also canned chutneys, relishes, beet pickles, and one summer we even tried some ketchup. The shelves in the fruit room were lined with colorful red, green, yellow, tan, pink, and purple row on row of all kinds of preserved foods. Tall Mason jar quarts of produce stood along with pints and small jelly jars. This was the place in the house where crocks, pressure cookers, funnels, grinders, slicers, sieves and large kitchen pans were also stored to accommodate all the canning needs.

Other main crops grown in the East View garden were beans and peas. In the early days all the vegetables were canned in quart jars. After we got electricity and our treasured eighteen foot freezer, they were blanched and frozen. This means they were placed in boiling hot water a short time according to recommended charts for freezing. For instance, beans needed to be scalded three and a half minutes. Immediately after lifting or draining the vegetables from the boiling kettle they were immersed into ice cold water, were cooled, drained thoroughly, and bagged in plastic bags. Water from the cooling pans was carefully taken outside to give moisture to the petunia flowers in a nearby bed. Before 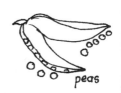 the freezer days all vegetables were canned using pressure cookers so the fruit room was the holding area for all vegetables too. Fruits and vegetables for the year's meals stood side by side on the shelves of the storage room.

The cave was another place where food was stored. It was located inside a sloping bank on a hillside southwest of the house. The two, slanted wooden doors of the cave opened to five steps which carried one down to a tall, wooden door. When the door opened into the darkness, a wonderful rich earthy smell immersed. The steps were cement but the stairway and the entire cave was lined with red bricks. The ceiling of the cave was domed and had an opening in the ceiling. This thick brown pottery chimney vent extended upward to the top of the hillside, which allowed air circulation inside the cave. As you entered the cave there were two waist high cement shelves on each side of the large room. On these shelves ripened fruit was stored. In the fall green tomatoes were taken from the garden before a promised frost and were laid on newspapers to ripen. Ripe tomatoes from the East View garden could grace a Thanksgiving table under perfect conditions.

The fifty degree temperature of the cave year round made it a perfect storing place for apples, carrots, squash and potatoes. The carrots were put in sand in a huge crock in the cave where they kept fresh and tasty as they could be. The potatoes were simply piled high back in the far corner of the cave where they remained useable all year. Lots of onions were also grown to full size in the garden and were harvested in the late summer, dried, and were stored in burlap bags or they simply lay on the shelves in the cave. Before electricity, fresh milk was brought up to the house in a small aluminum pail with a black wooden grip on the handle. The milk was stored in the cave on the steps along with butter and cream in the cooler months of fall and winter. Mom also made corned beef and other meat specialties and stored them inside crocks in the cave in the winter.

Of course, the fresh spring crops of lettuce, spinach, green peas, radishes and green pull onions were tops on the planting list in the spring. These newly picked specialties were prized. Mom especially liked new lettuce with a dressing we made with light cream, some vinegar, sugar and some cut up mild green onions. Nothing said spring like a green tender salad.

spinach

Maybe rhubarb sauce might though, or rhubarb pie or rhubarb crisp. Rhubarb grew in another garden spot just south of the house where the boysenberries also grew. When it was time to bake a pie or cook some sauce we would cut the fat tall stalks of rhubarb for a tasty super dessert.

radish

Along the fence of this garden was another spring specialty, asparagus. This treasured spring green prize was also grown along a fence from an old garden at the farm across the road we termed "the other place" or "Uncle Pete's place". Often, in the afternoon when the work inside the house was complete we would take a walk with a sack and paring knife and saunter behind the old house there and cut the fast growing green shoots.

There was a cherry tree in the orchard on "the other place" which was hit by a storm so there were not many years of cherry picking and pitting, but when it was growing, if we could beat the birds to those plump red prizes, a cherry pie was always the reward.

Apples were plentiful from the large trees in the orchard across the road and west of the house. The sauce, jelly, and pies made from the red fruit were enjoyed each year. Although one could not preserve the early spring blossom's beauty of all the fruit trees at East View in any way but pictures, their soft pink and white spring blooms enveloped the world around them in spectacular aromas and display. Memories of this caliber are stored and treasured for a lifetime.

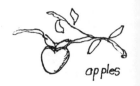
apples

One summer I remember Mom and I experimenting with making elderberry jelly from the long clusters of tiny berries we found on the sprawling vine along the apple tree from that old orchard. The white miniscule berries had to be picked, washed, boiled, and strained through a cheese cloth and finally made into jelly from the juice. We only did this once. Grape juice was  extracted in much the same way to make jelly or a Swedish fruit pudding called kram. The Swenosens, friends from a farm a mile north sometimes brought the excess purple grapes from their vineyard and we put them to good use in our kitchen. Grapes were much easier to handle because of their large size compared with the small elderberry.

grapes

Also in the orchard across the road there were a couple rows of black walnut trees. I remember some tries at gathering those black golf ball sized nuts and the labor of shelling them. It made for fresh walnuts but a lot of work. Squirrels usually had them all tucked away for their winter use before we had time to go looking for them.

Cucumbers planted in hills took a lot of room in the East View garden. Sliced cukes were a favorite of the summer time suppers simply sliced and prepared with a vinegar and sweetener. Most of the crop was made into pickles. It took a lot of plants to make batches of sweet pickles. Really good sweet pickles require large quantities of small cucumber fruit all at once to brine for several days so many hills were always planted. Dill pickles used the slightly larger whole cukes and bread and butter pickles were made from sliced large cucumbers or cukes as they were called. Mom always enjoyed varied tastes with her dinners. I think she had an innate sense of feng shui balance in her palate. She was always experimenting with various relishes and pickles and used their color and piquant tastes to embellish the food she served. Mealtimes were purposefully designed at East View and were occasions of importance.

cucumber

Mom even had horseradish. It was in the garden south of the house near the Wincharger tower. I remember one harvesting of this pungent root. Dad brought quite a bit of it in one afternoon. Mom proceeded to clean it and put it all in her blender at once. What a strong sensation! Scent-sational! Horseradish defies dry eyes! Lots of tears accompanied this experience but horseradish in cream was a favorite accompaniment to ham. Worth the effort!

Mom often tried different vegetables. I remember one summer she planted kohlrabi. We learned how to cook it but it never became a favorite. Zucchini was not popular when I was growing up but I am sure Mom would have had it in her garden if she had known of it and the many ways it could be served. Small Fordhook lima beans were a usual in Mom's garden. She always said she enjoyed the task of removing the beans from the pods after we had gone to school in the fall.

Mom always included some flowers in her gardens. Some of her favorites were zinnias, cosmos, marigolds, and her favorite, asters. When she looked up from her weeding and gardening, she enjoyed seeing the great colors of all the blooms. She liked the asters especially because when they were in their height of bloom she could bring in a bouquet on her birthday, the 25th of August.

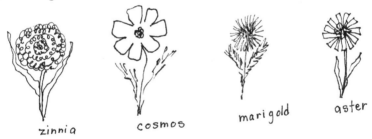

zinnia   cosmos   marigold   aster

Most of the vegetables we ate all year came from our gardens. With the cave, canning, and the freezer we were able to "put away" the majority of the vegetable and fruit needs for cooking for our family. The "fruit room" in the basement was the place where the jars of stored food were kept in multi-colored row upon row on the shelves built there. From the verdant level rows in the gardens and tall specimens of trees, came lines of colorfully preserved produce ready to use for looked forward to meals all year. Much of the food served at the table came directly from the soil, the plants, and the dedicated work of all the members of the family. Much pride was taken in producing and preserving the food grown at East View Farm.

REGIMEN

East View Farm activities followed a similar design each week. Many tasks were required to manage all the needs of the people who lived in the two-story, white four-square house. The family living there was multi-generational. Grandpa and Grandma Palmquist lived there as well as Dad's sister, Aunt Ruth when Mom and Dad got married in 1935. The complexity of the relationships could be overwhelming at times. It was necessary to keep the physical surroundings orderly and running well with systematic routines to make it as simple as possible. When three children, Charlotte in 1937, Betty in 1941, and Carl in 1943, were added to this mix it became even more multi-faceted. Eventually of course, Grandpa (1861-1943) and Grandma (1864-1947) died but then to add even more diversity to the people residing there add a boarding country school teacher for a school term or two and at times a hired hand. Life could be complicated but each day of the week had particular tasks. The necessary things to be done were broken down into specific responsibilities needed to be completed each day to keep everything running smoothly.

Monday

Monday was "warsh" day. It was not acceptable to do anything else on this day which was set aside for getting all dirty clothes clean. All fabrics used during the previous week were on the agitation schedule in the house at East View Farm on Mondays. Laundry duty reigned on the first day of the week. Until electricity became reality the only reason it would not take place would be the lack of enough electric current stored in the batteries down in the basement. If no winds were in the recent past weather conditions at East View, there was no capacity to move the blades of the Wincharger which created the electric power stored in the batteries. Most Mondays the washing was completed and every day thereafter followed its own routine schedule. Each day was filled with its own special activities.

Tuesday

Tuesdays were usually days set aside for ironing. Now before ironing could take place, the starched and some other items with extra wrinkles must be sprinkled. This meant the dry article was dotted with water from a small, coke type bottle with a corked round top with tiny holes much like the watering can used in the garden. The to-be-ironed piece would be spread on the white metal kitchen table, sprinkled, and rolled up tightly to get the whole item uniformly damp. Once this took place ironing must follow after a few hours of waiting for the dampness to reach all the fabric in the piece. If too much time elapsed because the folded roll was misplaced or the work was interrupted, there could be a musty odor and possibly mildew found on forgotten articles. This was true especially in the summer. Once ironed, the articles were placed on hangers to hang in closets and/or folded for storage in dressers until their next use. Sheets and pillow cases were stored along with blankets in the wooden built-in linen closet upstairs and fine white linens and table clothes were gently placed in lavender scented drawers of the buffet.

Wednesday

Wednesdays did not seem to have the important issue event of the other days. I don't remember any special routine occurrence on this middle day of the week. So many other activities took precedence at one time or another with all the work there was to be completed; I can imagine this was a day to get them done. For instance, spring and fall cleaning. Now these were days which took regular weekly cleaning to a whole new level. Walls were scrubbed, fixtures washed, windows were cleaned, and screens or storm windows were washed, polished, and put on or off depending on the season. Silverware shone and goblets clearly sparkled in the china closet especially before holidays or special company meals. Routinely rugs were taken out on the lines to be beaten until the arrival of the electric vacuum cleaner. All the nooks and crannies of the house were spruced up with days of heavy cleaning. In the spring, a day was needed to clean out the pipe to the chimney from the cook stove in the kitchen. Also in the spring the gardens needed to be prepared and planted, in the summer there was weeding, harvesting, and preserving of produce which continued into the fall. Perhaps if butchering was to be done it would be done on this day as it was a full day's project. On a farm there is no such thing as an empty weekday. Many activities besides regular house maintenance filled in the Wednesday slot.

Thursday

Thursday was another matter. This day was bread baking day: the day to make coffeecakes, cookies and cakes. Mom usually made Swedish rye bread and sometimes white bread. Her Swedish rye was made into three or four loaves with leftover dough going into a circle of flat bread which often did not make it even to the supper table. The fennel and anise of the rye bread baking formed a rich spicy aroma in the Thursday kitchen. The coffee cakes were formed from rich yeast dough with fillings of cinnamon, sugar, and often citron or raisins. The long rolls of dough were cut with scissors and twisted to form what looked like a braided top. These coffee cakes were a must with Sunday morning breakfast where a quick bowl of cold cereal was downed along with some coffeecake and cold cheddar cheese. The usual cookie Mom would make is the ever popular chocolate chip. Her cake specialty was a Throw Together Chocolate Cake. She was always experimenting with new recipes but these were the standbys she almost always had on hand. All these good bakery items were used and enjoyed every day at East View.

Even when Dad was working in a far field and could not make it home for coffee in the afternoon, Mom would pack a pail for him with some hot coffee in a Mason pint jar sweetened with sugar and some rich cream. She wrapped the glass in thick newspapers to keep it warm and help keep it from breaking with the hopping along of the young delivery people. Iced water in another quart jar, separately wrapped in more layers of newspaper, helped assuage Dad's thirst on the hot afternoons. Between the insulated jars she tucked some cookies and/or cake. It was our happy job to walk out to the field wherever he was and bring him his "coffee" in an aluminum pail. We were always met with a broad smile and enjoyed a few moments of quiet afternoon rest with Dad. This pail was also used to carry fresh milk up to the house from the barn after milking.

Once every month the local Willing Workers club met and I believe it was on Thursdays. It was a group of neighbors, mostly to the north who met for friendly exchanges. It was an afternoon of visiting with no agenda but friendship and catching up on the happenings of Concord Township and the world beyond. I remember one fall bazaar they held at Center School with baked goods for sale on tables along the western wall, some entertainment, and other events. It was so crowded the bazaar room seemed very warm. This was probably where Aunt Ruth was a lucky winner of a dark but colorfully stitched crazy quilt the Willing Workers had completed with scraps of suiting material from Hanson's Dry Goods Factory in Sioux City. Names I remember in the Willing Workers are: Townley, Falk, Carlson, Udell, Rental, Karrer, Olson, Hess, Bortels, Gard, Ladau and of course, Helen and Ruth Palmquist.

In the early summer the Willing Workers held a Mother-Daughter Event at one of their homes. It was a very simple affair with sharing of an Ode to Mothers and an Ode to Daughters. The ladies in this group had showers for their daughters and supported them as they began their life journeys. Mom was often in charge of their wedding receptions because she enjoyed organizing food and laid a beautiful table with her silver service. In those days, the serving ladies who loved to help wore fancy half aprons over their fine dresses. Weddings were simple matters at local churches with the reception downstairs with wedding cake, of course, punch, and perhaps ice cream, nuts and a special candy to serve. The table was decorated with flowers from the country gardens, simple but beautiful.

Mom loved to entertain and prepare her specialties but one day when she served her favorite dessert to the Willing Workers she was taken aback. The pastor from the Leeds Wesley Methodist church visited the Willing Workers one afternoon when it was at East View. Mom was serving her famous date cake desert she called Dark Secret. She served it broken up in small pieces on a large glass plate and over the bits of cake she poured a little pineapple juice and placed small crisp pieces of freshly chopped pineapple and slender slices of banana. Fluffy whipped cream topped the platter with some bright red maraschino cherries over the top for added color. The pastor entered the kitchen just as she was ready to take the dessert out for presentation and serving. He exclaimed, "My, what a good use of a cake failure!" I am sure the look on her face was full of chagrin but she would never let him know it as I can imagine her turning away quickly and going proudly into the dining room with her masterpiece. What did he know anyway??

Friday

Friday was cleaning day. If possible, each room was scoured with our rags dusting all furniture with lemon oil and the floors were either mopped (usually by hand) or in the case of the kitchen, scrubbed. All the rugs were hand vacuumed with a carpet sweeper. Everything on the tops of the bureaus and dressers in the bedrooms, buffet in the dining room, TV, and tables in the living room was removed to chase the dust settling there. Room by room, usually upstairs first, the house became clean and orderly. Every day the seventeen wooden, varnished stairs must be dusted so there was a lot of practice swishing a dust rag around at East View. Since there were many people going up and down, living in all the spaces, it created a bundle of activity and there was a lot of dust to eradicate.

If there was Missionary Society meeting at church it was usually on Friday. It was one event at church Mom would try to attend. Since Mom did not drive the car it was one of our duties to take her to this meeting each month. When you were fourteen in Iowa in the 1950's you could get a learner's permit and drive as long as you were with a parent with a driver's license. Mom had a license but did not drive so we got a lot of experience early in life driving Mom. It just was how things were done then and we never thought anything about it. When one knew how to drive a tractor, moving to the car was not hard to do.

Saturday

Saturday often brought the women of East View into the city to shop and go out to lunch at restaurants in either Martin's or Younker's Department Stores in downtown Sioux City. What a highlight for the week! I often remember ordering warmed ham sandwiches on toast with a soda for dessert. A ladies lunch supreme! The men at home were on their own to find their food. Lots of walking, talking, looking, shopping and enjoying time in town were the order of the day on Saturdays. It was a must to dress up with our good clothes, skirts or dresses of course, perhaps gloves and a purse tucked under the arm and away we would go. Spanorty was a word Mom coined and used in later years to describe the result of the preparation to look your best! When we went to Sioux City on Saturdays it was a time to do just that. The free parking lot for downtown shopping was at the large auditorium in Sioux City on Gordon Drive. It was a several block walk to the shops and department stores but we never minded the distance even carrying lots of packages. When we went to Sioux City on Saturdays it was a time to do just that.

After the downtown errands had been done, on the way home Mom usually had a shopping plan of going to at least three grocery stores to shop for the bargains found there each week. After carefully looking at the Sioux City Journal newspaper ads, Mom insisted on capitalizing on all the good buys. At the A and P Grocery or Skaggs stores in Sioux City, Mom brought a case of eggs each week into the back of the store and used the money to buy much of the groceries there from the egg money paid to her. She always insisted on the best produce she bought or cans with no nicks as she said the eggs she brought in were always candled and scrutinized for anything less than perfection so she figured the store should not be selling anything less in their other departments.

One of Mom's favorite places in the world was a grocery store. She enjoyed seeing all the varieties of goods there and prided herself on the prudent shopping she strongly encouraged we all learn. She loved making comparisons, looking for new baking ingredients and varieties of extracts, spices, condiments, vegetables, and fruits.

To complete an easy day, on Saturday night we usually had loose meat sandwiches on fresh buns from ground beef just purchased. Hamburger was slowly cooked with perhaps a bit of chopped onion and spices with a little water and ketch-up and placed on buns. A can of baked beans and some potato chips rounded out the meal. Saturday was a laid-back day in the East View kitchen. Saturday was "Lady's Day".

The day ended with baths and shampoos before bed. All water for a bath was heated on the stove in the kitchen and was taken upstairs to place in the bathtub until the late 50's when we got a water heater and then running hot water. Shampoos used rain water collected from the roof in a large crock on the north side of the house. The soft water in its natural form was also heated and brought upstairs to be used in the sink to wash hair. One by one, except Dad, we all were polished for Sunday. The house was clean, the baking done, the shopping finished, and it was time to look forward to Sunday, the day of rest.

Sunday

Sunday dawned early with a hurrying to get the chores done, Sunday dinner started, a cold breakfast downed, and Dad's bath completed so all could dress and rush to Sunday School and church at Augustana Lutheran in Sioux City. Often Mom would just stay home and prepare a wonderful noon meal in quiet. Whether she stayed home or not we always ate a special Sunday meal in the dining room with flowers or something as a centerpiece with a beautiful cloth on the dining room table. Bread was always passed first, then in order meat, potatoes, gravy, vegetables and any salad or other foods followed. Carl, my brother, often made delicious shrimp cocktail as a first course and we always had some special dessert. Mom loved to make Forgotten Meringue as a last use of her oven on baking days. Over this she placed some frozen berries she preserved from the summer plenty. Sometimes it could be as simple as whipped Jell-O, topped with a plop of rich, fluffy whipped cream served in her sherbet glasses but it was always something to make the meal stand out from weekday fare.

Many Sundays we had guests joining us and often we were also invited out to other homes. Sunday was not a time of work. Examples of some of the Sunday dinner visitors were Adolph and Agnes Hagland, cousins of Dad, Aunt Anna (Mom's sister) and Uncle Chet when they lived in Sioux City, Mom's cousins, the Johnsons, Dave and Hilda with their children Audrey and Harland were visitors. Signe and Axel Hallin were treasured older visitors. Sometimes a visiting pastor from Augustana was invited home for dinner. Sunday was a time to visit and relax. The newspaper was read always and many Sunday afternoons, Uncle Leonard, Aunt Hilda, and their children, Stanley, Bruce, Genell, and Lois came out to visit. Mom had usually made an extra Jell-O salad of some kind, had cold meat, homemade buns or rye bread, chips, pickled herring, assorted cheese and other light supper items handy to share. She always had her throw together chocolate cake or hot milk cake baked along with some cookies too, of course.

For the kids, it was time for PLAY! All seven of us Palmquist and Johnson kids played all afternoon when their family visited. In the summer we played baseball in the pasture with hopefully dry cow piles for bases. We sledded down the long hills in the winter. Sometimes Uncle Leonard pulled us behind a vehicle in a long string of screaming sled riders up hills and then down. We rode scoop shovels down the hill to the barn, careening into each other as we wildly slipped over the icy snow. After supper, we always played parlor games in the living room. Button, Button, Who Can Find the Button?

was one of our favorites. To play this game the leader hid a small object like a thimble or perhaps even a button somewhere in the living room while all the rest of us were in the stairwell going upstairs behind a closed door. When we came back in the room, if we got close to the hidden, but viewable object we were told we were getting warm. When we were almost on it we were told we were hot. The first person to find the object was able to hide it the next round. Can you imagine the noise of the search?

I think the favorite game was one where we all sat around in a circle on the floor in the living room after supper. This time it was one person who had to go out of the room away from the other players. The rest of us in the living room quietly designated one player in the circle to be a leader. This person led us in all kinds of activities as snapping fingers, clapping, tapping our heads, slapping the floor, or maybe a favorite which was hands flopping back and forth at ear level much as a donkey's ears would. The guessing person, who had come back into the room and stood in the middle of all this activity, had to guess who the leader was. We watched the leader carefully out of the corners of our eyes so as not to give away their identity. The guesser had three tries to name the leader and if the leader was discovered, he became the new guesser and must then go out of the room and it all began again. If the leader was not guessed, the poor person trying to find the leader had to leave the room and try again. It was always Uncle Leonard who led the game formation and played with us. He taught us the moves.

Uncle Leonard was a great story teller and in the summer, in the dark of the night on the front porch we all sat around in the warm shadows and his ghost stories never failed to delightfully frighten us. Oh how we loved Sundays with the Johnsons! One story in particular stands out in my memory. Uncle Leonard had all seven of us gathered around him on the front porch of the house and he began remembering another evening long, long ago sitting on the same front porch at East View. He recalled seeing and hearing two tall, large, black men slowly walking down the gravel hillside road which went by the farm. The pitch darkness of the midnight hour hindered any real vision of the strange men; the crescent moon's glow eliminated by heavy low-hanging clouds. The shadowy mysterious creatures slowly moved down the hill, the silence broken only by the crunching of their shoes in the loose gravel along the ditch. "It looked like one man had a small sack he held in his hand," Uncle Leonard recollected thoughtfully, "And the man with the sack offered something out of the bag to his walking partner. We could hear him say...."

"One for you and one for me, One for you and one for me, One for you and one for me." Uncle Leonard said it must have been peanuts or small pieces of candy they were sharing as they slowly came down past the farm.

All the way down the hill the sharing continued, Uncle Leonard's voice would get softer and softer, slower and slower. "One for you and one for me." One for you and one for me, One for you and ONE FOR ME!!!!!." This last ONE FOR ME uttered in a loud shout was accompanied by Uncle Leonard reaching down and grabbing whoever it was closest to his feet. All seven of us gasped in fear at first and then of course we tumbled all over the front porch in gales of laughter as we realized Uncle Leonard had fooled us. Oh what joy!

In the summer on Sundays Mom and Dad loved to take rides and leave the world of their farm behind. Sometimes it was to visit friends like a Danish brother and sister, Carrie and Harold Jorgensen in Sergeant Bluffs, or nearby friends and neighbors from Lawton, Lorraine and Roscoe Hess, or old Swedish neighbors, the Larsons who lived just one mile to the east. Signe and Axel Hallin were other friends who used to invite our family for Sunday gatherings. They were the closest people to Grandfather and Grandmother I remember. They had a beautiful dining room set* which I remember sitting at for many a fine Sunday meal. One Sunday evening in particular I remember Signe's cheese soufflé. This was a first for me and very impressive indeed.

The farm of Adolph and Agnes Haglund, cousins of Dad, was another favorite place to go. Agnes was a superb cook. Her Sunday dinners were out of this world in quantity and flavor. Good friends, Adolph and Dad would often enjoy telephone conversations together on rainy afternoons when they could not be out in the fields. Adolph had a droll sense of humor and was an avid gladiola grower. Visits to their farm north of Sioux City were always great get-a-ways.

On other more rare occasions our family would take longer rides just for the sake of going. I remember visiting Ponca State Park in Nebraska or at times just cruising in the area with the windows open enjoying looking at the world around us. Sometimes we headed north towards LeMars or east towards Moville. Dad was always checking the crops we passed by. As roaming was not a high speed activity, destinations were not as important as the traveling through the countryside.

Sometimes in the icy winter when no one visited we would play Chinese Checkers, Scrabble, Monopoly, Flinch, Old Maid, Rook or other games with Mom in the kitchen during the evenings. We especially enjoyed Flinch. She loved to make divinity or fudge on frozen Sunday afternoons. I remember even pulling taffy, one time stretching it from one end of the kitchen to another.

Weeks at East View were busy ones and full of all kinds of activities. Each week the pattern was usually the same but the weaving of the events made a rich fabric of life for all of us living there.

Now this Berkey & Gay dining room set is here in our home in Bristol, Illinois. When Axel sold his home and furnishings, Dad bought it. For many years in their home on the farm and on Court Street in Sioux City we enjoyed Mom's dinners around it. Now it is my privilege to have it in our family's dining room. The walnut and maple burl and English oak swirls provide great materials for the Jacobian design. Signe hand needle- pointed all the chairs with flower patterns of different kinds. For me, it is an honor to enjoy this beautiful antique set.

Throw Together Devil's Food Cake

6 tbsp cocoa	2 eggs
½ cup soft butter	1 cup sour milk
1 ½ cups sugar	
2 cups flour (ordinary wheat flour sifted before measuring)	

Beat mixture all together thoroughly. Then add ½ cup boiling water with 1 level teaspoon soda and 1 ½ teaspoons vanilla. Beat again—and beat, beat, beat. Bake about 40 minutes in a 325 degree oven.

Frosting:
3 cups powdered sugar
1/3 cup butter
1 tsp vanilla
2 tbsp unsweetened cocoa powder
3 tbsp warm strong coffee

Combine and spread on on top of cake.

Dark Secret

1 lb dates	1 cup sugar
1 cup walnuts	4 eggs
½ cup flour	1 tsp baking powder
2 tsp vanilla	¼ tsp salt

Mix and bake ½ hour. One hour before serving tear cake in pieces the size of a walnut. Spread on chop plate. Pour over this the juice from a *small bottle of Marashino cherries. Slice 3 oranges thinly and 6 bananas and place over cake mound. Over all spread whipping cream. Dot with Maraschino cherries cut in half and sprinkle Grapenuts cereal over the mound. Serve from the large glass plate.

(*recipe suggests a 10 cent size bottle)

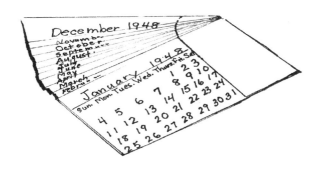

Duty Calls

Each day at East View began with chores and each day ended with chores. In between there were a myriad of things to accomplish every day. All of the work must be done. Animals depended on care and family member's well being was dependent on the carrying out of many responsibilities, not just on one day but every day. Duties called to be done not just in a five day work week, but seven days of every week, every month, and every season. The seventeen stairs in the house dusted by hand, meals and snacks prepared, dishes washed by hand in a white enamel pan in the single kitchen sink with hot water heated in containers on the stove were all examples of responsibilities which must be done. Everyday life at East View Farm was punctuated with jobs completed.

Every morning the cows were milked in the barn and were brought up to the pasture. Milking machines and equipment had to be washed and sanitized and the barn cleaned in readiness for the next milking session when the herd was brought back down the hill from the pasture and milked again in the evening. Ground grain scooped into five gallon pails brought into the alley in front of the cows enticed them to come in for milking. If there was not enough corn ground for the next day, the faithful John Deere was hooked with a long, wide belt to the grinder and corn was ground. It was stored in a small wooden red building in front of the corn crib.

Cows were not the only animals needing attention. Mom checked on her chickens every morning. They roosted each night on narrow boards stretched across beams about three feet high in a chicken house which was on the second floor of a red building south of the barn. In the level underneath the chicken house there were hog pens at one time. Every morning Mom walked down the hill from the house and up the wooden steps to let them out and make sure the hens had plenty to eat and drink. We bought large bags of special feed for the chickens on our Saturday trips to town along with sacks of oyster shell they needed to ingest to make firm egg shells. Long rectangular aluminum containers made this food available at all times. Tall round water hold-  ers were also available in the chicken house to provide a drinking supply and had to be kept filled with fresh water carried over from the faucet at the nearby milk house. Every night the doors to the chicken house were closed to safeguard the hens sleeping. In the morning Mom would let them out to roam as they wished. The roosters basically took care of them- selves, strutting around the barnyard menacing any invaders and scratching for treasures in the dirt. The hens busily clucked after laying their eggs and roamed at will during the day. The chickens at East View led an independent life for the most part.

The real difficulty for the chickens was when the raccoons would make the roosting, sleeping birds their meals if the doors were not closed. One year a raccoon came each night about midnight for several nights in succession to our second chicken house which was not as carefully guarded as the main chicken house. It was located not far from the garage. Many chickens chose to sleep there, especially the roosters. One spring, a raccoon started coming regularly. Each night she came she carried a screeching chick- en away to her den to probably feed her young growing babies. Carl was very young but had a gun and killed her. She weighed in at over forty pounds.

Another earlier time a raccoon had been prowling one night around the farm buildings and one of our dogs cornered her up in a tree in the garden south of the house. Mom and Dad devised a plan to kill this raccoon which was not easy since they did not have a gun. The sunlight barely crept over the horizon when they set forth their strategy. Mom was to stand at the bottom of the tree with a spade in her hand ready to club the animal when he came down and it was Dad's responsibility to get the raccoon to move. Dad used all kinds of means to frighten the raccoon so he was forced to leave his perch. The scare part of this preparation finally worked for Dad, but here it went wrong. Mom's job was to club and kill the raccoon with the spade. Instead, the raccoon ran down the tree and scurried quickly right between Mom's shaking legs and ran off home free. Such excitement! And it was not even day yet!

All the work of growing and protecting the hens resulted in the real daily prizes of raising chickens: the hen's very regular every day egg production. Predictable but problematic! Hens were not very cooperative in the sharing of their eggs! Our hens laid their eggs on straw in wooden box-like shelving units. There were two levels of these shelves on the south wall of the chicken house. They looked like containers turned sideways so you could see the determined hens as soon as you stepped into the hen house. The egg picker's responsibility was to get under the feathers of each hen and retrieve

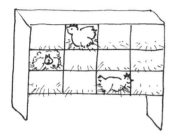 the egg without getting pecked with her sharp beak. Some of the determined old nesters had to have their head held down with a quick movement of one hand while the other hand slipped underneath to retrieve the treasure. My sister, Char, was known to throw one of her long legs up into the nest to hold down the hen's head and then snatch the egg out.

A large wire basket held the confiscated eggs and they were brought up to the house and down into the cool basement to wait for a washing, if needed, and candling at the end of the week. Candling was done simply with a light bulb in a round cardboard unit which allowed my mom to judge the contents of the egg for quality. When clean and candled, the eggs were placed in large wooden crates separated by slim folding cardboard dividers for safe transportation. A soft pressed indented divider for the eggs separated each layer. One crate could hold about thirty dozen eggs. On Saturdays they were brought to either Skagg's or A &P Grocery store to be sold.

Previously, I said the real prize of raising chickens was the eggs they produced. This is true. But the tastiest reason for raising chickens on the farm is the wonderful platters of substantial, rich meat we enjoyed from the young well-fed roosters Mom raised. Mom was a city girl but she quickly learned how to raise, kill and dress chickens. After catching the chosen one with a wire hook she had for this purpose, she grabbed the protesting zanimal by his feet and held him upside down. Next, she got an axe and quickly put the roosters head on a narrow stump near the garage which was always there just for this purpose. One determined chop and all was over. The legs held secure, the bird was held at arm's length to drain the blood. Soon the twitching stopped and the rest was history for the bird.

In the house a large kettle of steaming water was ready, much like the three pigs had for the big bad wolf waiting for him in the third little pig's brick house fireplace. After pouring the boiling water into a pail, the chicken was dipped into the hot water in the basement to loosen the feathers. After the feathers were pulled off unto some newspapers laid out for this purpose, the body of the chicken was taken upstairs to the gas stove where it was singed over the open flame to take out the pin feathers and small immovable remains of the feathers in the skin. Next the insides were carefully removed. The chicken was then cut into its serving pieces, and the only step left in the whole preparation process was a time for cooling the meat in the refrigerator. Friday or Saturday was the day when this activity took place so chicken could be served on Sunday.

The smell of chicken cooking in Mom's roaster is never forgotten. The large juicy meaty pieces of the free-range roosters made the modern small drumsticks and breasts bought in stores pale in comparison in size and taste. The creamy gravy made to go over the mashed potatoes served with the chicken was rich and succulent. Hens escaped such fate until they got older and were not laying eggs regularly. Then they were used to make stews and soups. The long cooking of the older meat made luscious broths into which homemade noodles or dumplings were cooked to go along with the chicken.

All of the noisy clucking and crowing chicken's lives began early in the spring when Mom would order her baby chicks, always a variety of white chickens called Leghorns. They would come to the Lawton Post Office in large cardboard boxes with lids separated into four units. After they were brought home to the farm there was a lot of excitement! Each box was full of little yellow fluffy powder puff like peepers. Their tiny beaks squawked loudly and they were taken up to the brooder house which was a small red wooden building west of the house near the orchard. A heater with a broad round aluminum hood hung in the center of the wood floored building and created a warm, nurturing place for the little puffs of light yellow cotton candy chicks. Mason jars full of water were turned over into special bases to provide water. Food was placed in low rectangular metal feeders which had small circles on their covers so the tiny birds could peck and eat the food but not get it all over. The little chicks loved to keep warm together and were only quiet when secure, warm, and full. They grew quickly. Mom carefully tended their growth and watched their progress with pride. Her chicken broods were prized by this city girl made farmer.

Another kind of chicken made its home at East View. Lorraine Hess, a neighbor and friend of Mom and Aunt Ruth, gave them some bantam chickens. These were small colorful birds which lived their lives outside of the hen house basically. They paraded around the barnyard in their brown, black, and red array of feathers, almost one half the size of the other chickens raised. The banty's eggs were very small and were not used for selling. These hens were particularly adept at finding hiding places for their brood-  ing nests outside somewhere or in the barn. These small chickens were origi- nally from Bantom, Indonesia. In the early seafaring days bantam chickens were procured by sailors to take on their voyages for their eggs and food supply. At East View we had Seabright bantams, developed by Sir Seabright in Great Britain in the nineteenth century. Bantams at East View raised their young on their own, teaching them how to hunt for their own food, scratch- ing for bugs and seeds in the dirt incessantly all summer. The barn mangers were home to many of these free-range colorful birds.

Another farm bird waddled around East View Farm one year. We had a flock of white ducks which made their way quacking and squawking one summer around the buildings. The flock started as a cute bunch of little  ducklings in the spring, but grew into a herd of traveling eaters and waste depositors. We tried to contain them with fencing but to no avail. Between the chickens and ducks it was hard to grow any flowers or plants of any kind around the farm. Their trampling and pecking made it hard for anything to bloom. The bills of these birds left only stringy stems to mom's treasured petunias. The trails of the ducks were not pleasant to walk through either. Not surprisingly, another flock of ducks was not found at East View the next summer.

Another kind of animal lived at East View for a short time. Uncle Leonard, Mom's brother, worked with a livestock commission company in the stock yards in Sioux City. He sold animals for farmers and ranchers. One spring a female sheep from the far western plains gave birth to twins down at the stockyards while she was waiting to be sold. Since the mom was sold the twins were mother- less. Uncle Leonard brought them out to the farm and we raised them on bottle milk. One of the twins became Snowball, a beloved animal but the other twin, Curly, grew four horns and was trouble to all he met. Snowball grew a thick coat of wool which

had to be sheared. I remember Dad removing her wool one day. Eventually she was given to our milkman, Durwood Hansen. His daughter, Leslie, relates that it was this gift which started her dad's interest in raising sheep on their farm just one mile north of us. The four horned fellow did not last long at East View. He loved to come up behind us and butt us with his horns. He was scary. He became some delicious lamb chops and roasts we enjoyed.

Pigs also have lived at East View. Pigs were not the main livestock when I was young but I can remember some years when pigs were raised. Their snorting and snuffing were always rather humorous. Pigs loved to cool off and clean up in mud puddles if they could find them. Usually they were in the yard south of the cow yard, but Dad put up pig wire and they were allowed to roam south of the buildings on the hillside. Pig wire is fencing with large wire rectangular holes which will enclose pigs. The usual barbed wire fencing would never contain these animals. Pigs loved to eat and would eat almost anything. Dad fed them a mixture which was like a red sloppy food of corn cobs, grains, and liquid. Boy, did they like to eat! And did we ever enjoy eating pork!

The event of butchering one of the pigs was looked forward to and also dreaded as it was a day of hard work. Lots needed to happen any day butchering was taking place. Usually the butchering occurred on a cool fall day. After killing the hog, the hog was raised up in the corn crib with the pulleys used to lift wagons. He was skinned and gutted which meant that the insides were removed and then the dressing of the meat could proceed. Most of the time mom and dad did all the cutting, wrapping, and freezing of the roasts, chops, and other cuts of pork by themselves. No hams or bacon were salted or smoked but all of the pork was used as fresh roasts and ground.

Nothing was wasted. I remember some delicious meals of new brains sautéed in butter. These were especially good on fresh white bread smothered with ketch-up. Another specialty was pig's feet. Uncle Leonard especially liked these. The fat of the pig would be rendered which means it would be heated to remove the lard and after the lard fried out there were cracklings left which was used along with some of the lard to make soap. We loved to eat those fresh crisp bits of rendered fat and could almost get sick from eating them. The lard was used for pies and in baking. The smaller intestines of the pig were salted down and saved for the making of a Swedish sausage called Potatis Korv. Mom liked to make another Swedish specialty called Sylta which used the pork hocks with a veal shank to make a jellied meat. The meat was cooked off of the bones with spices and when shredded was put in a container with the broth and cooled. It would make a gel-like meat which was sliced and served like a cold cut from a delicatessen.

When it came to larger animals like beef, a butcher was usually there to help. We ate everything from the steer just like the pig. I can remember baked, stuffed heart and a delicious meal of tongue simmered with a seasoned tomato sauce. Of course the liver was used. Ox-tail soup was another favorite. Sometimes Mom and Aunt Ruth made their own corned beef after butchering. The cut and ground-up meat would remain in a freezer at a local locker in Sioux City until it was brought out to the farm to be used. Even the hide of the animal was sold to Fairmont Dairy in Sioux City.

Calls to chores resounded all the time at East View. Always there was something to do. Duties called and working answers followed. There was no need for a list of "Things to Do". Things were just done. What was needed was completed. No choices. No thinking about it. Just done! And when the day was finished and darkness was closing in, there was a saying often remembered, much as Grandpa Palmquist had recited in Swedish each night when going up the stone steps to the house from the barn, "Another day closer to home."

Pasture Society

Power structures appear all over in human relationships. But people are not the only ones who vary in their need for influence and supremacy. The cows at East View Farm were no strangers to strong bosses and submissive behaviors on sliding scales from the very competitive to the ones who did not care at all. I guess one of the reasons we loudly called "Come Boss! Come Boss!" at the pasture gate each evening was to get the first leader or chief cow moving, then surely the rest would follow.

Every morning after milking was done, our herd of twelve or so large black and white Holstein cows would be escorted up the hill on a gravel road west of the buildings of East View. At the top of the hill there was a barbed wire gate on the right side of the road which led to the pasture. This enclosed grassy land extended to the western fence of Uncle Pete's original old farm and included the farm buildings which used to be Dad's home when he was a small child after the early death of his mother. His Uncle Pete and Aunt Betty were his mother's siblings and they operated this farmland east of Sioux City, Iowa. Mom and Dad purchased this eighty acres of land in the late 1930's to complete the original one hundred twenty acres bought originally in 1917 by Grandpa Palmquist and Dad.

A small creek with many springs flowed along some spreading willows in the valley of the pasture. An old swampy bog hugged the adjoining hill with rounded mounds covered with grass which would shiver when feet jumped from one hummock to the other. Each summer day the cows slowly ate and chewed their way across the meadow of grass and then cooled themselves in the muddy water of the creek on hot summer afternoons. Cows often lined up side by side with heads to tails, alternating, so they made good effective use of waving tails chasing flies from each other's fur.

Late in the afternoon when field work for the day was finished, it was always someone's job to go up and get the cows and bring them home. The satisfied and full cows were ushered down the hill and into a cow yard located just east of the barn. A large, swinging metal gate was closed behind them and milking time came soon. The cows were milked in a large, dark red building called a barn where many of the farm animals lived, especially when cold winter days came. Beside the barn stood a bright white milk house where milking machines, milk cans, and the milk cooler were housed. I guess the name milk house says it all. Grandpa Johnson, my Mom's father who was a carpenter, built the milk house.

Twelve stanchions lined the milking part of the barn and stood ready inside the double door entrance. The two long vertical boards of the stanchions held each cow's neck firmly and were all locked into place after the cows entered the eastern barn door. When it was time for the cows to be milked, they went to their own spot. Just like family members usually have a place at the table for dinner, cows have their own permanent position in the line-up in the milking parlor. Ground corn placed just inside the stanchions in an alley-way between the horse barn and milking area was the enticement for the cows to come in. The cows stood on a clean, flat cement floor backed by a long rectangular gutter which held any manure the cows produced while they were in the barn.

Just on the other side of a tall outdoor highway sign which separated the barn into two parts (more on this a bit later), one could find pens of baby calves. In the early days, these stalls were for horses to rest after their long days of field work but in the 1950's they were used to house young calves.

Teaching the newborn calves how to drink milk was always a fun task. We took a pail with some milk and put our hand in the milk so the baby calf could suck our hand and thus get some milk at the same time. Soon the growing calf would learn to drink the milk all by itself without a hand from us but they always enjoyed just sucking our hands whenever we put them into their pens. Cleaning calf stalls and installing fresh straw was always a rewarding activity. The old mangers in the front of the stalls were perfect places to place hay and grain for the growing calves. Our barn cats frequently could be found sleeping in them or underneath a banty hen often hid her nests. Little calves were not alone.

When it came time to milk, always, always even the cow's order of entry into the barn for milking was nearly the same except for days when the power hungry ones defied the strong heads of the herd. Blackie was first and either Old Clean Up or Caboose was last. Many cows had their own ranking, personality, and name. There was LuLuBelle, Stubb Horn, Ruthie and many more. The sketch below is a simple example of a stanchion arrangement for milking.

Two kinds of milking machines were used. One brand, the Delaval, milked one cow at a time and another milked two cows at a time. Before cows could be milked their teats had to be washed. A pan of warm water and a rag was always brought into the milking parlor, ready for washing the teats. It did not matter if the temperature was below zero outside and freezing. The cleaning must be done. Only then were the cups placed on the udders and the milking began. The cows usually accepted this
arrangement. Their full bags of milk were ready for release and they gave their milk eagerly except for some flighty cows which did not last long in the herd. Their kicking and resisting was not tolerated. One cow had to be milked with her tail pushed straight up to the ceiling by a very persistent and brave Dad who stood behind her to manage this feat. This made her legs unable to move. She never changed and was not long in the milking pack. Kickers were also devices available to curtail anyone from getting hurt from those hoofed feet but I never saw them used. The close relationship of a herd master and his cows was a constant twice everyday association and

positive shepherding proved much easier than constant power struggles. A small dark plastic radio in the barn was always turned to some very pleasant dining music program from KSCJ in Sioux City while we milked to sooth the cows and the people milking alike.

After a cow was milked, the milk was carried from the barn into the milk house where it was run through a strainer with a round cotton pad placed in the bottom. The warm, rich, white milk ran into metal ten gallon cans where it was stored overnight in a large icy cooler. Our milkman,  Durwood Hansen, picked them up in the morning in his trusty truck to take them to Sioux City where they were sold through a milk cooperative to dairies like Youngs or Roberts. Before electricity came there was a large cement tub which was filled anew with cold water each evening to cool the milk. One of the benefits of the modern milk cooler and its frigid cold water was the crisp watermelons we enjoyed eating after a day along its icy sides. It was also a great place to cool off in the hot summer by simply putting wrists into the water.

Every morning all of the parts of the milking machines were washed with strong, soapy hot water and rinsed. Each night they were simply rinsed well with cold water so they were milk free and clean for the morning. Uncleanliness was not an option. Milk inspectors came regularly and were scrupulous to a fault looking meticulously for problems. One time Dad had to put in more light bulbs in the barn, one for every three cows I think. Another time he had to put a division in the barn between the calves and the milking area. A friend of his, Ray Chaussee, a sign builder, supplied a thrifty solution with a large sign from along a South Dakota highway his company no longer needed. It fit perfectly between the cows and the calves. When cars drove from the east at night on the road toward our house, the reflective letters on the sign made an interesting glow in the windows of our barn from the headlights of the cars. At the request of the milk inspectors, I remember one time Dad had to go up to the windmill at the top of the hill behind our house and put cement around the cistern there to make sure the water was clean. Now our family drank the same water, but it did not matter. We even had a hot water tank in the milk house before we had one in our home. When an item was on the list of an inspector, it had to be rectified.

The milk inspectors came during the day so they were never aware of the chickens that were determined to roost in the barn above the stanchions of the cows each night. I am sure they would have made some sort of rule about the need for their absence if they did know. The roosters especially liked to sleep balanced high on the wooden connection in the walkway between the two sides of the milking parlor. The wooden stanchions stood in two connected sets of six, six cows on one side and six cows on the other side. Uncle Leonard was down talking to us while we were milking one Sunday night and he stood in this walkway with his new light tan Stetson hat perched proudly on top of his head. He did not notice the rooster poised on the beam just above him. Unexpectedly the large bird plopped some very unsuitable material on Uncle Leonard's hat and Uncle  Leonard exploded into a tirade for a few minutes on the value of this rooster. It goes without saying that Uncle Leonard was more careful finding his place to stand after this episode. It still is fun to remember how fast he removed his hat and the shocked look on his face. And a NEW Stetson at that!

 Chickens were not the only animals beside cattle that made the barn their home. We always had many cats and of course kittens. They enjoyed some milk in their bowl each milking session. Cats were needed and worked diligently on the farm to keep the mice and other rodents away besides supplying warm companionship.

In the early days of milking at East View, an old hit and miss one cylinder engine in the old granary was used to power the milking system. Over the stanchions vacuum pumps moved wooden parts. Rubber valves were on the ends of the moving parts on which a milking machine was hooked to pull the milk from the cows. Later, when electricity came to the farm, an electric motor created a vacuum. A long pipe was extended along the stanchions above the cows. Hoses from the milking machines were plugged into the vacuum and a metal petcock was turned to open the milking machine to the sucking action and milking could begin.

Cows were an important part of the life at East View from the early days through the 1950's. Long ago in the early 1900's the cows were milked and the milk processed in a cream separator in the basement of the house. A by-product left over from the creation of the cream and butter was used to make mash. Mash was a red moist food for hogs which was a mixture of ground grain and cobs along with the whey solution from the cream production. The cream made was sold to Swedish families in Sioux City. Butter was another product made and sold from the milk directly to clients in Sioux City.

One of the best regular customers for these fresh farm favorites was Mrs. Carlson who lived on Iowa Street. She lived next door to the Johnson family at 2010 Iowa street. Mrs. Carlson's husband was a stock yards man and his wife was able to afford the best of everything for their small family of three. Alma Johnson, next door, was a good friend. Her husband was a carpenter and not always involved in a building project, especially during the winter. She often got the leftover butter, eggs, and cream Mrs. Carlson did not use. The Johnson family of six enjoyed the fresh farm produce and Alma would order once in awhile for special catering needs she had. My dad delivered the products and must have noticed the beautiful daughter of Alma, Helen, because he married her many years later.

In the late 1950's our family decided to not go into the bulk milk production system which was required at that time to sell Grade A milk to dairies. Bulk milk was a modern way of milking cows where milk went straight from the cow into tubes and then into a cooled tank in the milk house. Milk was directly extracted from the bulk milk tank in the milk house into the truck delivering it right to the dairy. It required a large amount of new expensive equipment. We decided not to go modern. Dad still sold milk for dried milk for a few years in the early 60's. I think when Mom and Dad were putting us children through college; the cash from the milk and eggs was what kept them through some very lean years.

I have always had a soft place in my heart for cows. I don't know if it is because of their big saucer like eyes. It might be their plodding acceptance of everyday sameness. Perhaps it is the soft skin on their noses which so inquisitively searches for the greenest grass and biggest piles of grain. Sometimes this fascination with green would get them into trouble. I especially remember early spring ventures. It seemed like always during the Lenten preparation time for Easter that the cows would get themselves into places they did not belong and we would have to spend time to get them home from the creeks they were foraging by or where ever they had found other irresistible grass growing beyond their pastureland. We always ended up looking for them and chasing them home only to miss one of the Easter week church services because of their antics.

Cows varied personalities have continuously fascinated me. A cow's curiosity could get her in trouble but often was just part of her curiosity in the world around her. Maybe my interest in cows is the contented way they chew their food, and chew, and chew and chew. Four times they chew their food as it goes through their four stomachs to be digested. Perhaps the virtual size of the bodies of the cows held its own attraction for me. Also, the large splotches of black in their white fur or the spreading white in their black fur gave each one their unique coat. Whatever the reason, I have found joy in remembering their "mooo"ving ways.

I remember watching a cow give birth to her new born calf one morning. It all happened so very fast. Dad had me feel the back hips of a cow right before she was ready to give birth one time. It was soft and pliable. Nature changes the body so the huge calf can be released through its birth channel. This particular morning, the air was frosty still and the cow stood apart from the rest of the herd next to the chicken house in the other barnyard. Quietly and without a sound the enormous baby emerged from below her tail and fell to the ground. The membrane around the calf was still intact when the mother turned abruptly around and began to lick the calf clean. When I think about it, the calf born has a long fall to begin its life. Soon the new mother nudged the newborn up on its wobbly legs. It was not long before the baby was eagerly nursing beneath its mom.

Mother cows did not always have such an easy time. I remember one late afternoon early one spring helping my dad with a young heifer that was having a difficult time delivering her young one. A heifer is a very young female who has a baby calf. Sometimes they have them too soon when they are not fully grown themselves. Most of the time then they have difficulty giving birth to their baby calf. Holstein calves are large and long legged right away when they are born. The heifer we helped lay back in the west calf section of the barn near the south double door. I helped Dad reach in and put a chain on the trapped infant. We had hot soapy water to keep everything clean. It took awhile and some cooperative work with the little mom and my Dad but everything turned out ok and the baby was born healthy and ready to go.

In that same part of the barn I can remember some days when Dad decided it was time to turn some of our young baby bulls into steers. He used his trusty knife and with a slit performed the undoing of these unsuspecting male calves. No farm could exist with many bulls around. One bull was more than enough. In the later years, no bull was needed as artificial insemination was used. Bulls were scary. I can remember the pawing in the dust and powerful snorting of one huge one. Not my favorite memory.

On the good side, there was always one of these steers who would find their way to our dining table. In the late fall, when an animal was chosen for food, it was killed and butchered. The supply of fresh meat prepared by the butcher was cut, wrapped, frozen and stored at a local locker. Nothing was wasted. Even the suet, or heavy fat was used to make soap.

Cows were an important part of the economic development and way of life at East View Farm. Economic, because they were a consistent way of funding needs for the growing family. Way of life because so many activities of each day centered on the needs associated with having a herd of cows. Cow's domestic qualities made them mutually interdependent with the farmers who owned them. It could be described as an almost a symbiotic re-lationship, mutually beneficial to both farmer and animal. Anyway one looks at it, this four legged creature was a very important part of East View Farm's early past. Cows ruled like queens in their day, even the lowly Clean-up. Last in the herd to walk in the line-up of moving cows, last to enter the barn, last in the herd to be milked, and the last one eating and leaving the barn after happily cleaning all the grain swept to the front of her which was left by the others, she plodded through life knowing the real meaning of the saying, "The last shall be first."

Country School Days

Schooldays at Concord #6 always began with singing from the song book Together We Sing with everyone in every grade lifting their voices whether they could read the words or notes or not. From kindergarten to eighth grade, the students in our country school sang together and played together. After lunch, our teachers usually read chapters from a book to all of us as we listened after our play outside. One series of books I remember with special affection was about a pig. Freddie the Detective by Walter Brooks was fun for all of us to hear of his escapades. I am sure the list of books read is long but he stands out for some reason. All of us quietly paid attention as I remember.

Now when formal learning took place it was an entirely different affair than the central activity of singing and listening to stories by all in the room. The teachers at any country school presented lessons in all subjects, to all nine grades, every day. There was a kind of magic which must have gone on as the teachers themselves were usually just graduates of high school with a little training from Normal Teaching classes nearby. The Woodbury County Superintendent came by often to oversee what was going on in the school. The students graduating from eighth grade in the country schools needed to go to Sioux City to take a test for graduation and the country kids seemed to have no problem mastering the skills expected. Learning did happen! Constantly!

I remember a lot of things going on in school every day, all the time. Since all grades were together in one big room, I could listen to lessons all the way up to eighth grade topics even when I was in kindergarten.

In later years lessons taught to students below my grade level made it easy for review if needed.

The only other student in my class, Sandra Amick, came in second grade if I remember right. She had a brother, Gary, who became the fifth student in his kindergarten class which made it the biggest class at Concord # 6. Carl, my brother, was also in that class. My sister, Charlotte went through all nine grades of school at Concord # 6. The year she took the test and graduated was the year our local school was closed. The testing took place in Sioux City at the County Court House and took all day long to complete. The next fall after Charlotte's graduation was the year our school district was consolidated with the Lawton School system. It was 1951.

The building for Concord #6 was a white, wooden clapboard one room school. It literally was only one room. A large bell hung in the steeple above the entrance to the school. A long wide rope hung from the bell and was used to call time for school and the end of recesses. There was a partial wall in the back of the room where hooks were placed for us to hang our coats as we came in the door. A shelf stretched across the top of the hooks where we could place our lunches we brought from home.

The school sat in the middle of an acre of grass with some outbuildings on the eastern edge. You see, we did not have inside toilets. The boys had an out house and the girls had a similar four-holer at the far end of a small building which housed the wood and coal for the furnace. The furnace, located in the southwestern corner of the schoolroom, kept us all warm through the winter. It was the teacher's responsibility to get the fire started in the morning and keep it going all day, just one of the many things required of her. I am sure it must have been part of the older students work to keep the wood and coal handy for stoking the fire. It was also the teacher's responsibility to do all the cleaning in the school. Floor mopping work after the students left to go home had to be done along with lesson planning for the next day.

Country schools came into being as a part of our U. S. history. In 1803 the United States had purchased the western watershed of the Mississippi River from France. Provisions in the Louisiana Purchase required land to be set aside for education, one acre every two miles. The new territory also set up a plan for a grid work of roads which were built around every square mile when possible. Woodbury County in Iowa is a good example of the carrying out of this plan. With schools mandated two miles apart, no one had over two miles to walk. Near East View Farm, one half mile east was Concord #6, a one room school was also located two miles north, and one two room, with toilets even, two miles west called Center School which was kind of a community center. Schools stood on the corners of intersections around the Center School at each two mile interval. Center School served as the place in Concord Township where voting was done, graduations of township eighth graders took place, and bazaars and events of the local clubs were often held.

Each school had a parent as a director who was responsible for hiring and keeping the local school going. Often the teacher needed a place to live and it was the director's job to find a home which would house the teacher. I remember a teacher named Miss Kivedra who lived with us one year. She was from a nearby town, Anthon. Her brother or someone from her family would come each Friday or Saturday morning to pick her up and she would return in time for school on Monday. Mr. Gard, a local neighboring farmer, was in charge of the tax money and wrote the checks used to pay the teachers in Concord Township. Education in Woodbury County, Concord Township was definitely a community matter.

Inside Concord #6 one would always find the rows straight and orderly because they were all attached. There was a wooden bench for sitting and a wooden topped front where the school books were stored for each child. These desks were all held togeth-er with wooden boards along the floor. The desk tops had a circular hole on the right side for ink along side of the long indented pencil slot. The small desks placed in front and the increasingly large desks toward the back of the rows made it possible for the kindergar-teners to be always closer to the teacher and see what was going on. The teacher worked  from a table or her desk in the front of the room, calling up classes through-out the day. She had a large wooden desk in the northeast corner of the room. In the front of the room was a large blackboard which extended the full width of the room and was usually full of practice work, announcements, and assignments. Three large windows on each side of the school room sup-plied a lot of light. This was good because kerosene lanterns which hung between the windows were the only source of extra light until electricity came in 1947.

Now you can imagine the need for a lot of books at many different levels must be procured for learning to take place at all these grade levels. This was every family's responsibility. The cost of books and supplies came from the parents of the children in school. They were purchased at the Woodbury County superintendent's office in Sioux City. We were able to bring the books home when we were finished because they were ours. We had boxes of books in the attic of our East View Farm home. One cold blizzardy winter day I remember my sister, brother, and I made a library out of the books along with our own personal books. We attached paper checkout slips inside the covers and pretended we had a library.

A regular real library day was a celebrated day at Concord # 6. We had very few extra books in our school so the visit by the Bookmobile from the central library in Moville, Iowa was an exuberant day. The joy and excitement of going into this large moving room with its stacks of books just waiting to be read is hard to describe. The bookmobile was like a giant bus filled with shelves of books and had a check-out counter behind the driver's seat. After thoughtfully pouring over all the selections and checking them out, we climbed back down the stairs with large piles of books which we read from cover to cover and shared with each other until the next month's visit.

Authors like Lois Lenski and of course Laura Ingalls Wilder were favorites. The pen and ink drawings in these books are still indelible in my mind. Lois Lenski wrote and illustrated many books based on the reality of different children in other parts of the United States. Her Strawberry Girl was one of her classic regional stories along with another titled Cotton in My Sack which was a picture of life in the south. Laura Ingalls Wilder's many books were a warm telling of the stories in her life and those of her husband in the late 1800's. The early years of his life were told in Farmer Boy. My brother, Carl, read this book so many times he had parts of it memorized. Laura's retelling of her start in life on the Wisconsin forest frontier was told with the book Little House in the Big Woods. She followed this with many more stories in books telling of her life like Little House on the Prairie, The Long Winter, and On the Banks of Plum Creek.

The students at Concord #6 even wrote to these authors and got answers back. I am sure the teacher in that term has had a treasure all these years as I can imagine and hope she kept the letters. Biographies, mysteries, nature writing, how-to-do-it and all the many other kinds of books brought by the bookmobile expanded our world beyond our local farming environment. During the summer, the bookmobile continued to come regularly to the school site so it was an extra special treat to be able to read stacks of books at our leisure at home.

But, books were not the only thing treasured in country school. Many of the teachers had us memorize poetry. Poems like Hiawatha's "By the Shores" and poems of Robert Louis Stevenson like "The Swing" are examples of poetry we learned. I remember making poetry books where we wrote poems and illustrated them besides learning them. Days were busy at country school.

Along with the regular poetry learning we had two major programs during the year, one at Christmas and one at the end of the year which was followed by a family picnic complete with ice cream, a real treat in those days before electricity. Durwood Hansen, our milkman, delivered the ice-cream from a Sioux City dairy. It came out packed in dry ice. He bent the flag pole in front of the school one day when he backed around at one of these yearly deliveries. Before the picnic and time for play activities there was always a presentation of examples of our new knowledge. At these performances we used the poems memorized and recitations along with a play and some songs we had learned. A black cloth curtain was put up in the front of the classroom on a wire strung from wall to wall. The piano served as the hiding place for performers on one side and the teacher's desk on the other. One of the mothers, Isabelle Swanson, played the piano and we performed proudly to the limit of our abilities.

A song which I sang one year at Concord # 6 became an entry into a talent contest the following winter in Lawton. I remember I sang, "I'm a Lonely Little Petunia in an Onion Patch" which became an entry into the contest but I did not get to sing it in the actual competition. The clutch went out in our 1941 maroon Chevy on the way down to the Lawton school for the community "American Idol" event which of course LONG preceded the present day contest on television. Lorraine Hess, a family friend and neighbor, and Aunt Ruth had designed, cut, and sewn a costume for me with green crepe paper around my body and pink crepe paper extending from my neck. When we left home early the night of the contest on the Lawton stage, the dark air was quiet and frozen at minus thirteen degrees. As the old saying goes, "The Show Goes On" and our family knew the Hess family was expecting us to participate. We had worked hard with the sewing and practicing so the adults in our family had decided to go as it would have been disappointing not to be able to sing and compete after all the time and effort even though the night was extremely cold.

We were over two miles from home when the clutch went out and the car stalled on a long hill. Dad walked home alone. He could not get any tractors started in the frigid winter air so he harnessed up his trusty work horses and drove them to our stranded car with him in an open wooden wagon. He hitched the car to the wagon and pulled us home. His feet were white with the cold when we finally arrived back on the farm. Mom slowly warmed his icy feet with cool water at first, then warm, tepid water to get his circulation back. His feet were never the same. The choices for Dad were limited on that wintry night long ago. His family was always a priority to him and his concern and determination was only heightened by his knowledge of the rest of his family marooned in the car.

Life at country school definitely was not all lessons, writing, flashcards, memory work and listening. Because there was no running water at school, someone had to go get water from nearby neighbors. The tall older children took off with a large, circular stainless steel pail with a lid to get water. A smaller child often went along to help with this task. The walk was half a mile or so to a nearby house which was usually East View Farm, where water was procured and carefully carried back. The water was then poured into a tan crock which stood way in the back of the school on a table. It had a spigot at the bottom where we were able to get drinks in our own cups we provided.

Every lunch we sat at our desks to eat our lunch and then went outside to play. The only hot lunch I can remember was the brain child of one of our teachers who heated canned soup on a hot plate one cold winter. What a treat it was! We must have used our cups for soup bowls and then taken them home as there was no way to wash dishes there or modern disposable plastic dishes to use. Even the pot had to be taken to a home to be washed. Sounds like a lot of effort for one simple nutritional warm experience.

Recesses at any of the times our teachers deemed them necessary provided time for everyone to participate in all kinds of games and activities. On warm days, a favorite was Annie Annie Over. We threw a ball over the boy's outhouse or even the school when the big fellows played and when caught ....well, I cannot remember the object of this game. I can only remember doing it, running, and hoping not to run into one of the big guys. Actually, we ran from one side of the building to the other after the ball was caught and anyone touched by the opponents became a member of the team who had thrown the ball.

The younger students played Fairies and Goblins. Someone was a goblin and the rest of the "fairies" started on the stoop of the school. The goal was to escape the goblins touch. If he got you, you had to go hold on to the flag pole. If you held your hand out while touching the flag pole and another fairy touched you, you were released, free, and could run again. The goblin had quite a time to get everyone to be goblins. I think the fairies usually won.

Another game was Stoop Tag. The goal here was to get from the side of the school to the fence either to the east or north, depending on the goal of the day. If the tagger chased you and you got tired, you could stoop and rest and was free of becoming tagged. You were allowed three stoops in each game. If a tagger got you, you became a tagger and joined the chase.

In the winter we were often outside playing Fox and Goose. We made a huge circle in the snow and made paths in the circle like a pie which is cut. We stomped a small circle in the middle. One person becomes a fox and the rest are geese. The fox chases the geese and all have to follow the "pie paths". The center is a free zone where you could rest and catch your breath. There was no cutting across the snow. All had to follow the paths.

In the winter we also slid on ice which formed on melted snow water which collected in a low section near the northeast corner of the school. We powdered it with snow to make it slick and slid with our boots on as far as we could go. When the bell rang to bring us in I am sure a lot of fresh country oxygen was flowing through our lungs from all our activities outside. The after lunch story we all listened to was always a treasured time. One warm spring day I remember Nancy Grigg as a kindergartener sitting in my lap during one of these story sessions. I combed the burrs and knots out of her hair she had gotten during these playtimes rolling in the grass and joining in the fun. Eighth graders to the new little kindergarteners, we all got along together.

Nancy and her brother Bert Grigg were just two of the students I remember. Some other students were Loren, Marlin, and Yvonne Horsley, Cecil and Frances Horn, Sandra and Gary Amick, Peter Christianson, Marlis and Minetta Olson, Regina and Claire Thoresen, Jean, Lois, and Lowell Swanson, Janet Hess, Marie Vermillia, and of course, the Palmquist kids, Charlotte, Carl, and myself, Betty. I do not remember any discipline problems at Concord # 6 except perhaps me, but that is another story. Oh, and some disagreements between families which needed to be solved.

Sandra and I used to have our little tussles. I remember going home one day with my navy blue and white striped dress with what was supposed to be a gathered skirt, but when I got home this day the bodice had multiple pins to attach it to the skirt. There had been some disagreement which caused the origin of this large ripping. Sandra and I had challenged each other while getting on a metal circular piece of playground equipment, the only piece of playground paraphernalia we had at our school. Needless to say, I must have been the loser.

The Horns, Amicks, and Palmquists had a half a mile to walk together westward each evening going home. One day Mrs. Amick came to school complaining to the teacher about some name calling going on so the problem was solved by allowing Sandra and Gary to leave the school first. The five of the rest of us were kept after school to allow the Amicks to get a head start. This did not work well. The Amicks dawdled and the rest of us ran so we caught up and the taunting began again. Both sides were obviously involved in this problem.

The walks home in the winter took a long time, not because of the weather but the myriad jumps into the deep snow in the ditches along the road. We all tried to see who could bury themselves deeper into the snow. The closest thing to being angels for us in our young days was the impressions we made laying in the fresh snow with our feet far apart and our arms flapping up and down.

When the ice froze on the creeks we tested the ice and made plans with the Horns to come back and go ice-skating. This is something I never was able to do much to the amusement of my friends and family. Even on two-edged skates, my coordination left a lot to be desired. A professional ice skating show at that time was the Ice Follies. We dubbed ourselves the Ice Fallies. I was the best example of that kind of skating. We still had fun together and hurried home after our play to finish our chores and do our homework before supper. Mom's delicious hot suppers were especially enjoyed winter evenings after all the play and all the work was done outside.

One day when we were in school, trappers brought up a very large beaver which had been chopping down trees and building a dam in the Whiskey Creek which flowed on the bottom land not far from our school building.

They told us all about the beavers and they showed us their catch. We all had our pictures taken with the trappers.

Days in country school at Concord #6 were filled with sights and sounds of learning and play. Somehow it all worked. The children who attended school alongside Char, Carl, and I all became upright citizens and became successful in their own right. The spirit of cooperation which existed between the parents to make this experience possible was a model of good discipline for the students at Concord # 6. There were no excuses! Deport-ment even had a letter grade on the report card.

With the vast differences in ages and grades, cultures, sizes, abili-ties, concerns and backgrounds of the students all in one room at Concord #6, it might seem that learning would be difficult. This was especially true when one considers the age and experience of the new high school graduate teachers who often taught us. Instead of being a liability, attending country school proved to be a model of learning for all who participated. Perhaps the one room country school could be considered the prototype for non-graded educational experience which, in its purest form, is the most valuable way to learn when properly done. But, we will leave that discussion to the profes-sionals. For me, as a student in country school oh so many years ago, I have fond memories of playing and learning at Concord #6.

Game Guide for Concord #6

Fox and Goose

Prerequisites for this game are about three to eight inches of snow and five or more lively children. First, a large circle is stomped into the new white snow. Then pie shaped cuts are made with paths, much like preparing a pie to be served, leading toward the middle. In the center of the "pie", another small circle is trampled flat and smooth. Half the fun of this game is definitely the forming of these game perimeters.

Play starts with someone as a fox and the rest are geese. The fox is hungry and chases the geese. When a goose is touched he becomes one of the foxes pack and is able to tag others. The last one tagged becomes the fox for the next game. The center area of the circle is a safe area for the geese where they can flee when winded or tired of running. Round and round, through the pie paths, and into the center and out, all the players run with glee in the snow.

Annie Annie Over

To play this game a large group of children need a small building to throw a rubber, soft baseball-sized ball over. At Concord #6 we usually used the boys out house. There needs to be two teams for this game. One team starts on one side of the building and the other team the opposite side. The shout of "Annnie, Annie, Over" is called by the team throwing the ball over the roof of the building. It is then caught on the other side and the catching team runs around the building. The throwing team does the same. They also run to the other side. On the way, if anyone on the catching team is touched, they join the opposite team. Now the throwing starts again. The same rules apply. The catching team does just that and runs around the building trying to tag  as many of the opponents possible. One side obviously dwindles here and one team finally wins all possible people to their side. At Concord # 6 we all played this together. Kindergarteners through eighth graders together throwing, catching, running, tagging, and just having fun filled many a recess and noontime free time with this silly game. Can you imagine the little ones running with the big muscular lanky eighth grade farm boys? Scary! Sometimes it was not just the outhouse which was used to throw the ball over but the school itself!

Fairies and Goblin

The front stoop of Concord #6 steps was the center of many activities. Just south of the steps about thirty feet away stood a tall flag pole where the older students put up the flag each day. This area between the flag pole and stoop was the place younger students enjoyed this game. One person was the goblin, of course. The rest of us were fairies, running around until the goblin caught us and we had to stand by the flag pole. We always extended  one arm out toward the other fairies for if they could touch your hand, you were free to run again. It was a real tug-a-war with the goblin gaining and losing quickly, the fairies running wildly and screaming when caught with their arms flailing in the air hoping to be released.

Captain May I

On the east side of the white school building there was a slight grassy slope towards the fence line of the adjoining field. It was in this area we lined up by the school with the goal of getting to the fence line. A captain controlled all movement. The players had to ask to move. We had to say, "Captain, may I". When the captain gave us the command, we were allowed to take several different kinds of steps with an assigned number of steps controlled by the captain. For instance, we could take five baby steps, tiny one foot ahead of the other footsteps. We could take perhaps three scissor steps, with one foot crossing the other in a cutting fashion. The favorite big mover was the giant step which of course covered the most ground. Sometimes players tried to slip in some more distance if the captain was watching other players. If the sneaky mover was caught he had to go back to the beginning line. First person to the finish line got to be the next captain.

Ball and Jacks

On the porch stoop in the springtime and fall one could find girls playing with a set of small cross shaped metal jacks and either a hard golf ball or a small rubber ball. The levels of difficulty of this game increased as the play continued. To begin the game, the jacks were tossed onto the flat porch floor and then slowly were picked up one by one after the ball was bounced. Up went the ball with the right hand and then quickly the right hand picked up one jack at a time. The game got more and more difficult than the onesie's, as we called the turn when we picked up only one at a time. When it was complete we immediately would go into the twosies (two at a time), threesies, foursies etc. up to the total ten picked up with each bounce of the ball at the end. But this was only the start of the game. Another level was the same pattern but the ball had to have a Double Bounce. Another level was called Around the World. This time the ball was thrown up with your right hand, and then your right hand had to go around the ball and also pick up the required number of jacks. The Into the Cave level required the players to shove the jacks, after the ball was bounced with the right hand, under the palm of the left hand cupped on the floor nearby. At the Pennies in a Basket level, the player must hold the left hand high in the air, bounce the ball with the right hand and quickly scoop up the jacks and put them into the left hand which was the "high basket". One level had you picking up the required number of jacks with the same hand the ball was thrown with.

Two people played this game, each taking their turn. Whenever another jack was touched besides whatever number was required of each turn, the play stopped. The opponent then continued to try to complete whatever their level was during their last time of play. For instance, if the player was going for six of the jacks and touched any of the four left, they lost their turn for this round and started again at the same point when it returned to them.

I remember at the last level, the opponent was able to throw out your jacks. This could be disaster but game players were moderately careful as they knew their own jacks could be spread to who knows where by their opponent when it was their turn to make things difficult. This game went on and on, back and forth, as you may see.

Softball

Several games were played with a bat and a softball. I don't think any of us owned fancy catching gloves but this did not stop us from playing on the level stretch of grass along the road west of the school building. One of the favorite varieties of softball was Workup where one started anywhere on the lineup and worked their way through the positions with each out until they became batters. The rotation to hitting followed  this order; outfield first, base players and shortstop to pitcher, catcher, and finally to a batter. Each batter had a chance to go around the bases back to home and stay a batter. If this happened no movement could happen in the outlying diamond. There were up to four batters. This was an orderly game but one at which the older fellows excelled but must have allowed all of us to play.

Another form of bat and ball play was Five Hundred. Here, a batter was needed and everyone else was out in the field. The batter threw the ball up, hit it and the fielders caught the ball with points assigned to the kind of hit it was. If it was a fly ball, the fielder got one hundred points. A one bouncer was worth seventy five points. A two bouncer gave you fifty and a rolling ball added twenty-five points. The fielders kept track of their points and the first one to get to five hundred became the batter.

Pick-up

One of the favorite quiet indoor games was merely a set of ten inch tall, narrow, colored, wooden toothpick shaped sticks. The object of this activity was to pick up as many sticks as possible without moving the rest. This was difficult as the small rods were held with one hand at the bottom of the cluster of sticks to start the game so the fallen stack was complicated and concentrated in a small area. When a player moved another stick when playing, the opponent took their turn and picked up as many possible without moving other sticks. When the whole pile was picked up, the person with the most sticks was the winner.

Musical Chairs

A favorite indoor activity when weather did not allow outdoor activity was musical chairs. Chairs were set in a circle with one less number of whoever was playing. The piano music set the pace for the march around the inside of the circle of seats. When the music stopped there was a rush to get a place to sit. Whoever was standing was out, another chair was removed, and the play began again until there was only one chair left.
The final music played. Whoever got the remaining chair was the winner and it all may have begun again if there was time. Gales of laughter, proud sitters, and disappointed slower chair grabbers were just part of this game which we all enjoyed. This was not a quiet time!

Learning Games

Playtime extended into academics with games like spelldowns. We all stood in the front of the room and words were given from spelling lists to recite correctly. When improper spelling was delivered, it was time to go back to your desk and work some more on your list! Sometimes contests at the blackboard included math problems. There were lots of games with flashcards. Older students monitored many hours of practice with addition, subtraction, division and multiplication facts. When I look back, it has 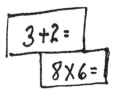 occurred to me that the older students got both a lot of re-enforcement of their skills and some even still could learn some forgotten facts when they practiced with the younger students in this positive leadership role.

Singing Games

Singing games often informally started during recess times and at lunch outside by the younger students. Ring Around the Rosy was often chanted while holding hands circling and when the all fall down came, we tumbled in a mass on the grass. We sang:

"Ring around the Rosy
A pocket full of posies
Ashes, Ashes,
We all fall down."

Another favorite was London Bridges Falling Down. Two people held their hands together between them high over head. Everyone else playing had to go in a line under the bridge they made with their arms until one of them was caught. The person caught had to choose which side of the bridge to go behind and hold the waist of the person in front. There could be a secret  choice of words to determine what side one would go on. To determine which side of the bridge you would go on you had to answer a "Do you like (?) or (?) better?" Examples of choices might be popcorn or cocoa, or peas or beans. This went on and on until all people had been caught but one. When that person was finally caught that winner could chose another person from the line with the longest number of people to be the new bridge. The game then continued. The song went something like this:

"London Bridges falling down,
falling down,
falling down.
London Bridges falling down,
my fair lady!(or gentleman)"

Seasons Change All

For the people in the Western hemisphere of our earth, time progresses in a very linear fashion; minute follows minute, hour gives way to the next hour, one day moves toward another, weeks go by, months race along into seasons, then into a year and years pass into decades, centuries and for some of us the millennium projects us into a new world of counting. We march forward. All moments move, point by point into the future.

In the Eastern Hemisphere of our earth, the way of looking at movement through time is very different. Eastern people have ways of thinking in which measuring and calculating the passing of time reflect a whole different philosophy. Occasions are placed in a more repeated or reoccurring way, circling and moving around and around. Nothing moves directly into the future but is on a progression of events like a spiral. In the world of nature time also moves in a more cyclical fashion much like the progression of phases as interpreted by our Asian neighbors.

On a farm, the work of agriculture follows the more circular way of recording changes. Agriculture moves through a series of growth sequences, harvesting, and then renewal. The stages vary throughout the cycle. There are periods of growth, maturity, and finally the gathering, only to start again and again, over and over throughout the growing season with each separate crop until the frozen winter seals the whole cycle. Then preparation is made for the new plantings and it all starts again. Round and round, over and over, the sequence repeats itself.

On East View Farm in the 1940's and 1950's, economic vitality was centered on growing and cultivating the crops of corn, soy beans, alfalfa, some oats, and perhaps some wheat. The presence of these crops insured not only cash for purchased necessities but food for the animals raised and grown on East View. All was intertwined. I remember some experimenting with growing sorghum but it never became a major crop. Grains and animals provided the background for the growth of the East View economy from the early 1900's through the 1950's.

Let's take alfalfa for example. It was an important food for the cows which were milked every morning and night. This milk sold provided cash for the family's needs. Every day the reality and necessity of this set of activities formed the perimeters of all the rest of the work at East View Farm. After the milking each morning and evening, the fresh, raw milk was stored in tall, metal ten gallon cans which were placed in cold water each night until an electric cooler was demanded by the milk inspection crews. The cans were picked up each morning by our milkman, Durwood Hansen, in his trusty milk truck. Rain or shine he drove into the farm along the barn on a wide dirt path, loaded the milk cans, backed around and left. He brought the milk into a milk co-operative in Sioux City which distributed it to the local dairies in Sioux City. Durwood was a large man and always came with a broad smile. He was so strong he could throw the full milk cans with one arm. We often teased him about the noise he made banging the cans around when he restacked them in his truck. He would always reply with a wink, "All the noise is how people know I'm working."

In the early formative years of East View, milk was churned, butter made, and both the butter and cream was delivered directly to mostly Swedish customers in Sioux City by horse and buggy from the Olson (Uncle Pete's)  farm across the road and from the present East View Farm. Dad and Grandpa made the trip into the city most Saturdays to directly distribute the eggs, chicken, cream, and butter to the waiting kitchens. Incubations of chicks every year provided flocks of egg layers, fresh eggs, and roasting chickens for the tables of many city customers. This provided cash.

Now the cow's food in the summer time was the green pasture land found at East View. In the winter it was a different story. Alfalfa or hay had to be grown for winter food. The hay could be red clover or alfalfa. It was used in the winter to add with grain to keep full milk production. Alfalfa matured three times every summer. Dad cut each crop with a #5 John Deere sickle mower pulled behind his trusty 1936 John Deere. The sweet smell of the new mown hay refreshed the senses like no other aroma. As it air dried, an Emerson Branington five foot bull wheel powered mover made in Rockford, Illinois, raked the hay into rows. It was used behind the Ford tractor to draw together the tiny round leaves and small green stems into furrows where it completed the drying and waited for the gathering. Before Dad's purchase of his John Deere in 1937 with its spiked, steel wheels, all hay was cut and gathered with the use of horses. There was a stacking device which used horses also prior to my time and memory but the one I remember was a real help in hay storage.

Before Dad had the baling machine, in the 40's he had a large, wood-tined stacking device which was put on the front of the John Deere. Many long prongs of wood slid along the ground under the rows of mowed and waiting furrows of hay until a large load was assembled. This overshot stack-er and hay buck was called a Booster Buck. It was developed and made in Dunlap, Iowa in l946. After the long prongs of wood gathered the hay, the load was then brought to a waiting person on a haystack. The alfalfa load was raised and pushed off the stacker and the person on the stack formed it into a great, tall, rounded square mass of hay.

Later in the 50's Dad purchased a compact piece of equipment called a baler which replaced the stacker. The baler packed the alfalfa into large, heavy rectangular bales of hay which were secured by baling wire. Dad's Minneapolis Moline Bale-o-Matic wire tie baler must have been a real vocabulary development machine. Sometimes it seemed like the time used to fix it equaled the time it actually successfully made bales. When a field was finally finished, a large flat hayrack was driven around the hayfield to collect the bales. Driving the Ford tractor when the bales were picked up was always fun. It was one of the few jobs I was able to do in the fields. These

bales, stacked under the high gambrel roofed haymow of the barn, provided food for all the cows through the winter. A ladder of boards ascended from the front of the cows much like a painter's ladder and after the climb it was very satisfying to pitch hay down to the waiting hungry cows.

Many other bales which did not fit in the haymow were used to feed the cattle out in the cornfields for the winter. They were stacked and fit together carefully to form enormous tight geometric, rectangular haystacks. The pattern of the bales laid was very purposeful and particular to form the sharp sides and secure corners needed to withstand the cold northwest winter winds off the Dakotas.

Although hay was harvested three times each summer, this was not true of the grains like corn. This crop needed all spring, summer and into the fall to complete its life's growth. In the spring the corn was planted once the ground was warm and workable. Dad used a lister behind his Ford to plant two-rows at once. A lister worked like a plow using what was called a double moldboard which was a curved plate of iron between the two plowshares. The plowshares turned over the soil and heaped the earth on both sides of the plowshare. Dad's lister was combined with a drill so he planted corn in the same operation. Before he planted he used a disc and/or a drag to break up the old stalks of corn left from the previous years. A disc was an implement which had many sharp, steel circular discs which cut into the leftover materials. The discs broke up the soil and readied ground for new seed. The drag was a lighter affair with steel prongs which were drug over the soil. Sometimes plowing was necessary first when a field like alfalfa was changed to growing a grain crop. When plowing the earth was literally dug into by turning it over with two large shiny plates which the tractor maneuvered deeply through the soil.

Before Dad purchased his tractors he used the work horses to guide him through the fields while he sat behind them on a corn check planter and guided the team of horses. We always had two large, brown work horses which were housed in our barn at nighttime after their day's work. Two I remember were named Nick and Daze. Their harness hung behind them on the west  wall of the barn. The front of each of their stalls had a manger where oats was measured and a large bin along side of the manger where hay was piled. I remember Dad working out in the fields and coming in with the horses but have had to rely on some research from a farm collector sight on the internet and some hints from a farmer friend to know what kind of implement the check-planter was which Dad was using in those early days with his horses.

Check-planter systems were designed to place corn in a checkerboard fashion, each about the same distance from its immediate neighbors throughout the whole field being planted. A wire was strung in a straight line all along the field to be planted with knot like spots placed at even distances of forty to forty two inches along its length. The check-planter followed this wire and when it passed one of these nodules, three corn seeds were planted at once in what is called a hill. When the row was finished, the wire was moved forty to forty two inches over and the planting along the wire and knots was repeated. Every row was at equal forty to forty two inches apart and every cluster of seeds was placed at equal forty to forty two inch intervals. This wide width was utilized as it was the breadth of the work horses used.

With a check planter a field could be cultivated first in the direction it was planted, later it was cultivated 90 degrees the other way, and finally it was laid by in the original direction. Laid by means the corn had reached a  height where no more cultivation could take place. At the turn of the century, this check planter implement was widely used with horses and later check planters were made for use with tractors. The later models had eighteen inch intervals. They were still being made as late as l952 when the International Harvester Company was still making the Mc Cormick No. 240 Two-Row Check-Row Planters.

Dad was still using a horse drawn check implement to plant corn in years which my sister, Charlotte, can remember. She relates Dad tying the reins of the horses under his arms and behind his back so he could work the levers of the machinery and off he would go back and forth up and down the rows. Some of the later implements Dad used to raise his crops were a Minneapolis Moline corn planter. He used a New Departure cultivator to keep the growing corn plants free of weeds. He used a John Deere end-gate seeder to broadcast oats. One of the jobs we could do to help with crop work was filling the seeder with oats as it spread the oat seed. I also remember over seeding alfalfa on an oat field with Dad. He drove the tractor while I was behind in the wagon with the seeder keeping it full of the miniscule brown alfalfa seed.

In the heat of the summer, the time of laying by the corn was always a welcome relief. Every year the war with weeds repeated itself. I remember the velvet weed or button weed with its soft green leaves and interesting burr formed in the fall. Cockle burrs had a detested olive shaped seed pod which would stick to anything moving by like animals with fur,

our trousers and our socks. Sunflowers projected their yellow heads above any crop and seemed to defy extinction. Creeping jenny and morning glory crawled along the black soil trying to create their own colorful green carpets. All sorts of grasses like the fox tail added to the crop confusion. Early in East View history Aunt Ruth wrote to Uncle Wibs about Grandpa's and her battle with morning glory in the east field along the Big Whiskey Creek. She relates the manual toil of using hoes to eradicate the rampant weed before Dad came along with his horses and cultivator to work digging out the rest of the weeds still remaining in the field there.

My favorite memories of tractor life can be traced to following the listed rows of corn Dad put in with the Ford Tractor. I can remember days when he was cultivating and had all three of us kids, Char, Carl, and I, with him for some reason. He had one on his lap and two standing at his sides along the fenders. I remember singing songs as irreverent as this Chinese man song...

In China once there lived a man
His name was Chingerly, Chingerly, Chang,
His head was big and his body was small
This little man had no sense at all
Chingerly, Chingerly, Chang
Tra la la la a happy man
Hiscoll and biscoll and champio
Hollopy, Wollopy Chineo

Now I can imagine if there were any neighbors close enough to notice we must have made some kind of impression if one could hear above the din of the tractors. However we had no complaints. In the days of the horse drawn work Dad had reported having a chance to talk to his neighboring farmers at the end of the rows when farmers shared news with each other over the fences while giving their horses a chance to rest. With modern tractors, one had no need to stop machinery with time to listen and share. On this particular day the sound of the singing from the four of us on that gray Ford tractor must have been something like the sheer joy of coyotes reflected in their howling to the moon for no particular reason other than the sheer delight of the experience.

The corn crop sprouted in the springtime and grew all summer. Eventually it tasseled, shot large cobs, and by the end of the growing season dried and turned gold like the treasure held hidden in the husks and brown silk.

Late in summer or early autumn through part of November after the corn grain and stalks had dried it became time to pick the corn. Dad had a 1949 John Deere 101 corn picker which went through the fields picking two rows at a time. The corn cobs were carried in wagons which brought in the harvest to the corn crib. The corn was dumped into a waiting John Deere Bucket elevator metal conveyor system of buckets and chain which lifted the corn into the sides of the giant wooden corncrib located below the house near the barn. The slats in the corn crib construction allowed the corn to complete the drying necessary for good storage. The tall corn crib was built from state of the art John Deere plans in 1918 .

Here the corn stayed until ground for feed for cattle or sold. The corn that was sold was shelled, meaning that the kernels were removed from the cobs. It would be later in the year when a huge, noisy shelling machine and its operator would be hired to come and the grain would be separated from the cobs. The corn went to an elevator via a large semi-truck and was sold. The cobs formed a pile of useful burning material to help start fires in the large wood and coal burning furnace in the basement to keep the house warm and to start fires in the cook stove in the kitchen. The cobs went directly into the house through a basement window where they were stored in a cob room built in the northeast corner of the house.

Unlike corn, soybean production was not a crop used in the early days, but it was introduced in 1951 or 1952 as more uses for this round, pale pea-like grain was found. Dad grew it and built two aluminum bins just south of the cattle yard to store this grain. Some perhaps was stored in the wooden bins high in the center of the corn crib.

In the old days when horses were usedfor transportation oats was grown by farmers to feed them. People in Sioux City at that time bought oats from farmers to keep their teams fed much like going to a gas station today. The oats and/or soy were stored in two deep room-like areas high to the north and south of the elevated assembly in the corn crib at East View.

The hard part about growing soybeans was the manual labor created in the summer time when weeds needed to be removed by hand. It was not laid-by like corn when it got too high to cultivate. Our family would attack the rows with sharp large machete like knives, cutting the tall sunflowers, bristly thistle or whatever towered over and grew hidden in the fat green rows.

Sometimes on a day with the wind blowing over the field one could almost get seasick with the waving lush plants bending and shifting as far as the eye could see.

Harvest of the soybeans was done by a combine. Dad got his first orange Case A 6 combine in 1950. I remember it well. Late one August, Aunt Ruth took the three of us kids into Chicago on the train and then up to Marquette, Michigan on Lake Superior for a vacation at Uncle Wibs and Aunt Amy's cottages (Wa Ni Pa) there. First, we were all over Chicago with a very brave Aunt Ruth to museums, zoos, and shopping riding to all the destinations on the elevated trains. What an adventure! We stayed at Uncle Wibs and Aunt Amy's parsonage attached to Gethsemane Lutheran Church where Uncle Wibs was a pastor. Then we continued by train to the Upper Peninsula. Mom and Dad must have had their own piece of heaven at home on the farm where they peacefully honeymooned without all of us around. I remember coming back to the farm and in our absence they had purchased a new Case combine and a new Mercury car! I believe it was a maroon 1950 car. The combine changed the face of oats harvesting and was the machine used to harvest soybeans.

Oats was never a main crop on the farm. Its importance was as a food for the animals like the horses, calves and milk cows. In the late 1800s and early 1900's oats was important to the city people to have a source of food and bedding for their horses. It was probably one of the reasons the Olson Brothers and their father had initially invested in farmland in Concord Township. In those years it supplied fuel for transportation needs. No gas stations were needed then but their horses needed fuel and it could be grown on near-by farms and used for very renewable energy.

In the 40's and 50's oats was used mainly for the farm animals. It was planted early in the spring from a small metal spreader located in the back of a wagon. As one person drove the tractor through the field, another person in the wagon was responsible for keeping the large hopper on the spreader attached to the end of a wagon full of seed which was broadcast throughout the field. The oats quickly germinated, grew, and by July the grains turned a golden hue. It was time to cut the grain and bundle it much like the small replica pictured here. This was done with a binding machine which tied the long stems into large, tall bundles

80

with twine. The bundles were then piled into upright sheathes of eight to ten bundles stacked with each other throughout the field. The upright shocks of oat bundles allowed the oats to dry thoroughly and the rain to simply fall through the bundles without damaging the grains.

At harvest, a threshing machine with a cooperative group of farmers who helped each other, moved from farm to farm getting their oats harvested. The farmers brought their hayracks (often pulled by work horses), collected the oat bundles, and brought them to the waiting massive thresher which separated the golden grain from the grassy like bases of the plants. These stalks turned into what was called straw and was extracted from the thresher to form into a cone shaped stack or later baled for use as bedding for animals in the winter.

The wagonloads of oats were brought into the corncrib. The wagons were lifted by ropes on the front wheels so the oats dropped into the waiting conveyor system and wide rectangular buckets lifted the oats upwards to be stored in the large wooden bins above the center of the corncrib. To get oats to feed the animals, a long wooden shoot about a foot wide extended down from each overhead room with a sliding handle at the bottom which could be slid to allow grain to fall down into the waiting bucket and then be slid closed. At the center of each overhead bin a large shoot was found where trucks could drive underneath and the whole bin could be emptied. This was used when the overhead bins were filled with soy beans and it was time for them to be sold.

The highlight of each threshing day when the grain was harvested was the noon meal prepared by the lady of each house. It was with pride that each farm woman fed the crew with her best and tastiest food made from her favorite recipes.

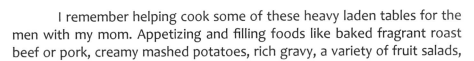

Outside the back door there were stations of water, towels, and soap set up so the men could all wash off the morning grime. They came into the houses spruced up as much as they could be after long mornings of work in the sun to eat at long dining room tables.

I remember helping cook some of these heavy laden tables for the men with my mom. Appetizing and filling foods like baked fragrant roast beef or pork, creamy mashed potatoes, rich gravy, a variety of fruit salads, vegetables of all kinds from the garden and of course fruit pies like apple and cherry and perhaps some chocolate cake to top it all off. Lots of cold water and/or tea were served with the food along with coffee for desert. Food was plentiful and flavorsome and of course the men's chatter was appreciative and happy, neighbors helping neighbors.

Life was good even in the outside sweltering work of gathering the harvests together. No comfort of air conditioning was found to escape to. Before electricity there were no fans even to help cool the very warm kitchens. The ovens and stove-tops ran hot preparing the foods for the heaped bowls and platters of provisions waiting for the men but it was all taken with the thought that that was how things were and was accepted.

And so the seasons revolved; planting, growing, and harvesting over and over again. With harvesting complete the cycle does not end but begins again with planning for the next period of growing and harvesting and preparation of machinery and tools to execute plans. A rich circle of life repeated round and round again, over and over, with unending growth, life, harvest, death, and renewal. Always changing, never finished, endings become beginnings with promises of growth to come.

Playtime

No electricity, no television, no computers, no video games, no electronic devices, no iPods, no DVD's, no CD's, no organized park district t-ball, soccer, softball, flag football or any other recreational classes, no cell phones, no text messaging, Facebook or tweeting, no skateboards, no swimming lessons, no oh so many things common today. What, you may say, was possible for children in the old days without all these things?

Life in the 1940's and 1950's did not depend on things bought or borrowed or scheduled or chased or demanded. For my sister, Char, my brother, Carl and I brought up at East View Farm, all days had chores which must be done but also during the days and evenings there were long stretches of time when we essentially played with whatever was at hand depending on the season.

In the winter we enjoyed building snow forts and throwing the usual snow balls and making snowmen. Occasionally the drifts down by the corn crib got so large we were able to form large caves inside. We burrowed back inside the white wind driven snow with shovels in two separate places. Then we proceeded to connect the two dugouts to make a kind of U shaped hut. We sometimes used burlap to cover the entrances and we sprinkled straw over the snowy floor inside. It was surprising how warm it could be within the darkened rooms.

One spring evening I remember walking up through the East View fields to a farm a mile north the first day of May. The Thoresons lived there,

Reggie and Cakkie, who were neighborhood friends from country school. It was May Day and we had made a May basket of mayflowers from the cemetery west of the house and had some chocolate chip cookies we delivered in a folded construction paper container Mom had helped us make. We hung it on their door and quickly knocked. We hurriedly ran back south through their buildings and on our way home. If they caught you, you would be kissed and we thought we were pretty cagey to pull this one off without being noticed in time for them to reach us. It was a long walk on a cool, fresh, spring night for such a task, but we had lots of sweet satisfaction and joy in escaping their catching us.

Mayflowers flourished early each spring in the Swedish cemetery just to the top of the hill past the orchard on our farm. They grew quickly. We looked forward to picking some every year and watched carefully for their blossoms. After a good rain and some early spring warm sunshine they poked their soft round stems up through the prairie grass with small, light lavender, tulip shaped blossoms. We searched each year among the tombstones and the old building site of the Swedish Lutheran Church which once stood there for their sure sign that spring was here at last. The blooms did not last long. One just had to be vigilant to catch their early brief flowering.

The three Palmquist kids were always doing something. Most of the time we were into some kind of play or mischief. Play, in its essence is the exploration of real life by youngsters. One day, I remember playing "funeral" with my sister and brother. When I think about the "game" it was not really a game at all but a learning to deal with a reality which had just happened in our lives. I was probably just 6 at the time, my little brother Carl 4, and our big sister Char, 10. We lived in a home with Grandparents and an aunt besides our parents. The time of this play is so real to me and must have occurred after my Grandma Betty died. I remember Grandma's sickness, helping watch over her with Aunt Ruth. I recall a visit from Pastor Evert praying the 23rd Psalm and the Lord's Prayer with the adults in the family at Grandma's bedside. When her body was taken from the house out the front door by the funeral director from Sioux City, I remember sitting and watching from the kitchen while this was going on. Reality is sometimes hard.

Later, though, I recall now the playing out of this all; one of us three went to the piano and played with no particular pattern at the bottom of the white and black keys. No song corresponded with the somber low notes we smashed away at on the piano in the living room. The serious noise must have represented death and while it was sounded at the piano, one of us was pulled out of the room, moved along the floor lifeless. Permanent events like death cannot be hidden from children and we were fortunate to have parents with the patience to let us work out our experiences in our play.

Most of the time when we were growing up, we played at home. One of our favorite things to do in the summer was make mud pies. We took this whole concept to a new level one summer when we decided to open a restaurant. We used to have our chef's kitchen over behind and to the east of the garage between two large trees. Usually we had a bakery but one ambitious day we decided to enlarge the concept to an eatery with eat-in dining. For a restaurant menu we had to devise much more than pies, cookies and cakes. We made meat pieces, peas, mashed potatoes and an assortment of other foods and coffee. Cakes were always the favorite to make as we decorated them with blossoms from low growing weeds at the edge of the fencing  of the near-by pig pasture. The pig-weed growing there had lovely yellow flowers which we cautiously picked from the prickly plants and decorated our cake tops. Other foods were pretty simply shaped according to the food type. For the coffee look we pulled dark brown seeds from another weed and soaked them in the sun-warmed water. The mashed potatoes we made had an interesting consistency and though definitely not the correct color, were an interesting addition to the diner's plates.

The clay for making mud pies was carefully mixed soil and water. We mixed it in large cans to just the right consistency for forming our foods. The baking was done in the sun on a plank placed just for this purpose. While the food was "baking" we made penciled menus, cut plates from paper, used twigs for utensils and set up a counter with a plank over some high saw horses for our patrons to sit and order. The chairs were cut up logs big enough for people to sit along the counter. What proud entrepreneurs we were when we enticed Mom, Dad, and Aunt Ruth to come and order from our new venture. They came, they ordered, and they enjoyed the event almost as much as we. At least, we thought they did. At least for Mom the three of us had spent some days out of her kitchen so her work went along uninterrupted.

One summer, after the shelling of the corn from the corn crib and it was empty, we decided to use it to make a circus. We got the idea from the two swinging ropes which had a loop at the ends which were placed around hubs of wagons to lift them. When the front of the wagons went up, they emptied their contents out the back into elevators which lifted the corn into the two sides of the corncrib. We often enjoyed just swinging in the cool breezes which swept through the central area of the crib. We imagined a trapeze show on this particular day. We set up some games, a fortune teller, and had other ideas. This did not all come to fruition as I remember, but we certainly had fun thinking, planning, and doing some set-up, even if we did not carry it all out entirely.

Outside the corncrib on the east side, an old hit and miss one cylinder engine powered the elevator inside before electricity came to the farm. It was connected to the apparatus inside with a long, round metal bar. This engine and bar were no longer used after we got electricity and were the perfect height for doing skin the cat and other acrobatic tricks we enjoyed playing outside along the crib.

The summer sun spread long hours of sunshine and shade at East View. We lounged and played our way through the hot days. One of our favorite places to fool around was between two mulberry trees by our garage. Dad made a swing there. He put a long sturdy pole across the two trees. It must have been a pole which had rotted in the ground and was replaced, left from the lines of a telephone company Dad and surrounding neighbors owned and kept working.

To make the swing, Dad first placed the pole, of course. Don't know how he lifted it so high above his head. But Dads can do anything! He made some heavy rope from twine and a rope making device. He strung twine from one side of the barn to the other, back and forth on hooks there just for this purpose. After stringing the twine through the rope maker he continued the winding of the long strands into a thick secure rope. The first swing he hung from this rope was a tire.

We would fling ourselves up in the air, jump into the tire, and wrap our feet around it. Later he made a regular swing, with two ropes and a smooth board we sat on. He must have needed to make more rope for this one. We spent many hours swishing back and forth in this swing. Is there any more joyous freedom than swinging high, swooping back, with the wind sweeping around you????

West of the house on the hillside near the Wincharger tower there was a group of giant purple lilacs. Someone planted several of them in a circular shape. When they grew tall, the branches grew together to form a thick roof over the inside of the circle. When we were little, this formed a perfect place for a playhouse in the summer. We swept the dirt "floor" with a broom and then Char and I gathered some of Mom's old orange crates and some boards to create some furniture. When we had everything built, we brought our dolls in the enclosed area for many an afternoon of play. Sometimes we brought our tea set up for a special party. We had wonderful afternoons in the shady room inside the lilacs. Summertime was a favorite time.

In June in northwestern Iowa, the weather is just about perfect. The sky on the prairie is often full of billowy, puffy white cumulus clouds. Giant masses of vapor stretch across the blue dome on the bright sunny days. The rounded tops of the white heaps of heavenly whip cream mound and move into shapes only a kaleidoscope can dream of. The front porch steps of the house at East View were the perfect place to imagine what all these shapes could be. The dream of floating through the sky on the top of these super, soft, cottony sky ships still comes back to me as an adult. Skies of brilliant blue were the standard in Iowa Junes.

My birthday occurred in the summer in July. On one of my birthdays I was very surprised by the gift of a bicycle. Char had a large bicycle which came from Mom's friend, Helga in town. It was an old maroon bicycle but very able to contend with the gravel road which went by our house. When Mom and Dad took the new black and brown bicycle out of the car for me on my birthday I was so excited. We named the bicycle, Elmer. He was the center of many adventures. When Aunt Ruth was feeling brave one day she decided to ride it. She ventured down the hill of our drive-way and turned right unto the gravel road. She turned too hard and kept going into a thick pile of gravel along the side of the road. This was too much for the wheels to maneuver. The bike flipped. Aunt Ruth rolled into the long brome grass in the ditch. She picked herself up, shook herself off unhurt, but exclaimed that she was not ready for bicycle riding anymore.

One time I had a similar experience. I was riding down the long hill west of our house. I should have had the good sense to slow down sooner, but as things often happen, I turned into the drive-way too fast, skidded on some loose gravel, and ended up on my knees in the grainy small rocks. A small, deep opening ensued on my right knee. It was so deep; a clear liquid began to flow from the sight. Just a little frightened, Mom took me to the doctor, Dr. Ackerman. She was a friend of Mom's and Dr. Ackerman fixed me up in no time in her home. We just did not go running to the doctor often in those days, so this was a new experience for me. I was glad to be on my way again.

Often on summer weekend evenings we ventured outside. In our front yard, we had a brick fireplace Dad had made where we often had hot dog roasts, cooked hamburgers and other picnics on Saturday nights. We brought a card table down for the food and sat on picnic chairs. Dad had some horseshoe poles to play horseshoe near-by. Often in the summer evenings we played workup baseball on the hillside and threw softballs in long throws along the barn below. Another favorite game to set up and play was badminton.

One night, near the picnic area we put up an old large tent from Mom's friend Helga, in Sioux City. It was a dark, grayish-green, heavy canvas tent and had flaps but no screens. I can remember big plans we three children had of sleeping all night in the tent. One of the particular first tries ended relatively soon after the sounds of the night became unbearable. Owls hooting, raccoons howling, small rodents scurrying, and all kinds of scary scenarios imagined in our heads kept us awake. As the lights of the house went slowly off, the rural black darkness encased us. One by one we retreated back into the safe confines of our bedrooms in the house. At least I know I did.

In our play we loved to get into large projects. One idea often led to another and away we went. One winter, down in the basement, we decided to make a grocery store. We gathered food materials from the fruit room, labeled them, priced them and made shelves to show them. Boxes were turned on their sides to showcase specials. I am sure Mom was not happy to have the would be "store keepers" mess up her fruit room where she had stored her food supplies for the year. I know she must have been not just a little agitated at getting boxes piled all over the one side of the basement, let alone the problem of the quart jars of her prized pickles and fruit plastered with our childish labels. This project was short lived as the clothes lines above the "store" were needed for the next Monday's wash. I don't remember cleaning it all up. I am sure Mom and Aunt Ruth were not happy with this undertaking but it was tolerated without too much fuss as it must have kept us busy for hours and hours.

Another idea we had one time was to develop a library from our books. Our family treasures books so we got many for presents for both birthdays and Christmas. We also had many books left from the textbooks we used at our country school. Since they had to be purchased for us and were not supplied we had boxes of them up in the attic. We decided to make our own library by gathering them all together. We made checkout slips and pasted in date slips inside the covers. Now this was not the best idea for some of the fancier books, none of the books really, as it defaced them. But, the Palmquist kids pursued their newest scheme and we developed our own library.

We used this library in what was probably our most often used play setting. Playing school had to be one of the favorite things we did on a winter day inside. I am pretty sure Char was the teacher most of the time. We had a great time. She had lots of papers for us to finish, flashcards, books to color, and activities to do. I think she enjoyed correcting it all too. We all became teachers in our adult life. It should not have come as any surprise when I remember how we loved to role play school in our younger days.

Oh the messes we must have made for the adults in our house! When I think about all the clutter we must have created with our projects we used to get into I am surprised we were allowed to be so creative. I do not remember the clean-up as well as I remember the actual activity. The time I remember Mom getting the angriest at us was a June day after a heavy rain. Each year, sometime between Aunt Ruth's birthday on June 13 and Dad's birthday on July 8th, the heavens opened up to some torrential rain and the bottom land east of the house would flood.

For some reason one morning after just such a rain, the three of us ventured down through the bottom field just east of the farm along with Dad surveying the damage. Dad must have walked back up to the buildings and left us to continue our adventure. We started stomping through some of the smaller puddles of water and mud. Then we found a large pond of water. We splashed and sprayed each other with much glee. Soon we were all wallowing in the water and mud much like some hippopotamuses do in their African setting. The dirtier we got the happier we were. Laying in the water and plastering each other we lost all training in décor and behavior. We became one with the mud we lay in. But then we realized it was time to go home. We looked at each other and kind of realized we had gone too far. It was only when Mom appeared at the door when we came back up to the house did we know how much in trouble we were. She had steam coming from her ears, her hair stood on end, from her mouth spewed words of condemnation, and the old vision of conniption fit could aptly be applied here. We were sent to the basement to take everything off and cold showers were applied to try and begin to make us clean again. It was the intervention of Aunt Ruth that saved our lives that day, I am sure. Who washed those muddy, filthy clothes I do not know. Maybe they were just thrown away.

Each winter we played lots of card and board games together and enjoyed picture puzzles. Char and I loved to play jacks on the hardwood floor under the mirror in the living room just outside the kitchen. I especially remember Old Maid and Flinch games. Puzzles on the dining room table were a must on snowbound days. Oh, I remember another day when Mom had just had enough of our noisy disagreements while playing. We three were inside all day on a frozen, blizzardy day off from school. I can remember we had gotten into some kind of tussle about one of these puzzles or games in the dining room and were running around the house. We had a perfect run around: kitchen, to hall, to living-room, to dining room and back to the kitchen. We circled round and round with some loud whoops, yells, and taunts. Mom had a wood pile stacked by her cook stove. Her verbal warnings had gone unheard. We did understand her status when we saw her with the first board she picked up from that wood pile. It had a nail in it. She threatened us sternly and was ready to apply it to our bottoms if our ears refused to listen. Things got very quiet then and we probably went back to our puzzles or game on the dining room table or whatever other activity we had going before the foray of the chase.

Spring, summer, fall or winter, it did not matter what the season was we three were busy with some kind of play. In winter, besides skating we loved to sled down the long hill behind the house. We started up by the Windcharger tower just west of the house and ended up in the trees down in the front yard. The long rides there were great but the excitement was to be found on the steep hill from the yard pole by the house down to the barn. It was too short to go on a sled as you would just bump into the milk house but it was perfect for the wild rides we had on a grain shovel. We sat on the metal portion with the handle between our legs. Off we would go, spinning and twisting our way down the hill as there was no way to steer a scoop. Where we would end was not important. The exhilarating zigzag ride was.

Sledding in the winter was great but it was also a time to build forts and have snowball fights. Fat snowmen decorated our farm yard. We also loved to make angels over and over in the snow, angels in form only I am afraid to report. No real ones at East View Farm!

In the fall I can remember making another hideaway much like the one in the snow drift when we hollowed out a tunnel in a stack of straw across the road. Leaves were another great thing to play in during the short fall days. We had a giant elm tree by our driveway and a lot of trees in our front yard and orchard. We never had to gather them or rake them into piles and collect the leaves for burning. On a farm you can just leto the wind blow them where ever they wanted to go. So we piled them, jumped on them, threw them around and watched them fall with glee. Fall was a short season in Iowa.

Play with our pets was another joy in our life. We had many cats and a procession of dogs. The first and favorite was a beautiful collie. We called him Laddie. His markings of white, black and brown were classic. He disappeared one Fourth of July weekend we spent up in Sioux Falls, South Dakota with Dad's cousin and wife, Ray and Edith Olson. When we got back we were so sad to not find our beloved dog. The next day we drove all over with Aunt Ruth looking for him. No one had a word about any sightings. Sure, we had other dogs, but none like him.

We did have lots of cats. One of the favorites of mine was Petunia. HE was a large, long-haired, black specimen who enjoyed traipsing along anywhere we went. He loved to be wrapped like a fur piece around the neck. Now you may ask about HIS unconventional name. As a little kitten HIS masculinity was not yet discovered and he was very playful around the lavender petunias near the back door of our house. Hence, he got the name Petunia and it stuck into adulthood. He was very adventuresome. I remember one time he must have been chasing rodents in the corncrib and had climbed to the top of the crib. He must have not cherished the idea of going down the same way but he did find his way out onto the roof of the corncrib. He meowed there for a day, a night, and a day. We thought he had enough sense to find his own way down, but no. There he sat. He no doubt became cold and hungry. I put a tall ladder up to the edge of the roof and coaxed him down to me. What a purring thank you he exuded! He was a great friend.

Petunia was not the only cat. We had many on the East View cat genealogical chart. One I remember fondly was a multi-colored one called Grandma who was a hunter extraordinaire. She proudly brought back some treasure almost every day it seemed. I especially remember her often catching even garter snakes she would proudly haul back to the house to show. Muggins was another white favorite among many more generations kitties who lived with us at East View. The dog and cats lived outside and they all liked to pile together to keep warm on the steps by the back door of the house. They would all sleep together and eat together the leftovers from our table inside.

After our days of work and play, our family's weekday suppers were served in the kitchen. The radio was usually on which played some dinner music which supplied the background there. After electricity came to our house our family enjoyed hearing many broadcasts on the large radio which stood on the floor in the chimney corner of our kitchen. We were avid and regular listeners of several programs. We would gather on the floor around the radio or sometimes just listen from the table. In the morning we often would listen to "The Breakfast Club". At noon the local KSCJ station had a farm program with live music which was enjoyed. Art Linkletter and his "House Party" was a favorite of Mom's as well as "Queen for a Day", "Fibber McGee and Molly", "Amos and Andy", Jack Benny, and other comedy shows brought a lot of laughs. Then there were the western shows like "The Lone Ranger" with his friend Tonto and mystery shows which kept us in suspense. The sound effects and voices helped us create our own pictures. It did not matter if we did not see anything. Our own brains all had their own visions going. WGN in Chicago had Saturday night country music programs we enjoyed also. After supper we always had devotions from a small monthly booklet of readings for each day which we got from church. Dad always read until we learned how to read and then we took turns. After devotions, we all prayed the Lord's Prayer together.

It was not until we went to Chicago for cousin Marilyn's wedding in 1947 that we saw TV. After we got our own TV in l950, life was never the same. We watched it with the aid of an antenna placed atop our Wincharger tower to pull in two channels which came from Omaha. Speckled, gray and white spots called snow was often the picture we saw but we still enjoyed this new phenomenon. Oh, how we grew to love this medium! Howdy Doody, Arthur Godfrey, Milton Berle, and the vast world of so many people associated with this new media extended our world in many ways. We watched after school before chores and for an hour or two in the evening after supper. At one time it was a fad to put a colored sheet of plastic over the screen, blue on top with green on the bottom to simulate "colored" TV. We could never dream of the pictures in high HD and sound we receive from today's sophisticated networks on our large theater screen systems.

An important part of our life at East View was our attendance at Augustana Lutheran Church in Sioux City. We attended Sunday School there, went to Vacation Bible School each summer there, and grew up attending the youth group activities through high school. When I was young the girls my age even had a Missionary Group, TAMS, Teen Age Missionary Society. Confirmation each Saturday morning provided us with understanding of our faith and a place to grow in our knowledge of the Bible. One summer for VBS all three of us stayed in Sioux City with Aunt Hilda and Uncle Leonard and their four children. For a week they endured the seven of us, fed us, got us ready and to VBS on a city bus. This gave us a week of new perspectives on life in the city. We learned to take a bus to church. The neighborhood on Virginia Street where they lived was full of children and we had a great time playing and going to the near-by swimming pool.

We had a great time growing up with our cousins Stanley, Bruce, Genell, and Lois. We were together most holidays along with Aunt Hilda's family which included her mother, father, brother and family. Larry, one of the Johnson's cousins from nearby Nebraska became another "cousin". We were always relegated to the "kids table" and that is where we wanted to be anyway. Sunday afternoons we were often together. We grew up playing all sorts of games under the leadership of Mom's brother, Uncle Leonard. He led us in all sorts of outrageous escapades. To this day, I do not know who had more fun, the big kid or the seven in his Sunday afternoon pack.

When I was ten and we moved from our country school to Lawton Consolidated School. Two new opportunities opened up to me there besides attending a class room with ALL FIFTH GRADERS! I joined the Banner Plan-nerettes, a 4-H club of young girls. The older girls in high school had a similar 4-H club called the Banner Planners which I moved up to as I got older. We met every month and learned about all kinds of projects, food, home care, decorating, gardening, and other things I found interesting. We had projects which we took to the county fair. I still have a picture frame I refinished by taking off about five layers of paint. The first year I did a demonstration with one of my new friends, Judy Pilcher. I still have a copy of it. It was all about floral arrangements. Judy's mother wrote most of it for us and we presented it, using real flowers. I also remember a two layer chocolate cake I made with a special seven-minute frosting recipe Mom had cut out of a Better Homes and Gardens. Our extension advisor thought it was pretty special as it was not sticky. I still use the recipe. Some of the lessons learned so long ago have stayed with me. Those are called time-honored and true.

Another activity I became interested in was playing the clarinet. When I first got to Lawton, they started pupils on band instruments in fifth grade and I selected the clarinet. Char had taken piano lessons for many years and I always admired how she was able to play those keys and memo-rize pieces for her concerts. Dad and Mom purchased my long, black, keyed "licorice stick" from an old church friend and the rest is history. I played all through high school in band, in quartets, trios, and soloed once in awhile for contests. We had large massed band festivals in at Morningside College where the whole gym floor was filled with northwestern Iowa band students. What a great sound that was! But it was just the beginning of life beyond the farm and the old country school.

In the summer the high school band played a short concert every Friday night in Lawton. After we played there was a free movie on an outdoor screen for everyone to watch in their cars and on some benches in the front. Ice cream cones were but five cents then at the small corner grocery store and my favorite soda made at the drug store was a cherry coke. The drink was made from red thick syrup mixed into the icy bubbly soda water from the large spigots behind the counter. Delicious!

When you are young, it seems as though life can go on forever. The days stretch out in what appears like an endless procession of events. Time is not a factor. At East View Farm, we were given many priceless treasures in our opportunities to have fun and grow as we were maturing. A balance between the chores and farm work was leveled with periods of the sheer joy of play. So many things are learned from the responsibilities of tasks and participating in the actual workings of a farm but equally important lessons are learned in the creative, imaginative use of free time.

Remembrances - Dad

A sifting of reflections
on a blizzardy night while
trying to say good-bye to
one who was loved so dearly*

love in reality is the
true actuality. It lives
on into eternity....

We love because God first
loved us... as a
father loves his
children.

I remember Boompa as we affectionately called Dad after grandchildren had renamed him, on one cool sunny March morning long ago. I must have been home one Easter week enjoying some time at East View during a spring break from my teaching days in Rockford, Illinois. Dad and I were riding, or driving, as a farmer would say, the small gray Ford tractor around the lower curve of the hill that led to the "Other Place". The other place was our farm across the road. A fence line separated a pasture from the field near this winding trail. On this particular morning a meadow lark was sitting atop a fencepost. This first herald of spring's entry was perched in solitude. Its breast was bulging upward. Its beak was pressed toward the sky. The key in the tractor's ignition was turned off. In the silence of that sun filled morning, Dad lifted off his red brimmed hat, sifted his hand through his hair and we paused to hear the song. We both listened and heard the lyrical cascade of the lark's song cast into the crisp morning air. Boompa is now somewhere in the intervals of the meadowlark's call, in the waiting moment of anticipation that forms all of God's eternity.

Often after the chores were done on Sunday evenings, Dad and any of us kids around would often take a walk up to the top of the hill behind our farmhouse and check the water in our well. The field that we walked through was usually planted with alfalfa and oats as the top was high and the fields slanted off on each side with steep slopes. One summer night I can remember from the rest. We often looked down over the vast vistas of the rolling hills beyond to the east and to the west but on this particular night we all laid down side by side on the top knoll and looked up together into the sparkling black space we call sky. The dark dome was illuminated with myriads of stars twinkling like huge windows into the beyond. We sorted these bright lights into constellations by simple names. Boompa is now part of that universe, set off in time and space but in the larger sense of being with God.

I remember Dad in the winter, breaking frozen creeks with an ax for cattle to drink water, bringing the cows in and milking them at their own special stalls every morning and night. Each day he did the ordinary chores that made his life the extraordinary one it was. The dependable care that he gave each one entrusted to him separated Dad from ordinary shepherds.

The gift which Dad gave to people was time. He always had time for anyone who had a need, a helping hand, or to talk. There was always patience for his three kids. We often followed him in a procession that must have been comical with me following in the rear calling out, "Wait for me! Wait for me!"

One particular day I can remember all three of us piled on his tractor as he was plowing on the bottom as we called the field below East View's buildings. One of us was by each fender and one was between his knees on the seat. We spent the whole morning singing songs he had taught us. Rituals each day were a part of our life. We took turns when Dad was done with his day's work to loosen his laces from the rivets on his dusty work boots. remember devotions each night after supper. We shared the day's lesson from the small publication called The Family Altar and then recited the Lord' Prayer together. Meals usually began with grace except for breakfast where it was not always possible to eat together. "Come Lord Jesus. Be our Guest And let these gifts to us be blessed. Amen." Church was an important focal point of Dad's life. We attended regularly.

The European ethic dad lived out in his life was to build something bigger than himself. All the small seemingly common place things he did were all steps in completing his dream. Dad and Mom together carved out of the prairie, a farm. With their own hands they built the reality of a vision. As immigrant's children they were united in their zeal to create an empire beyond themselves. Their hands are a testimony to this effort. Their knuckles have strained beneath bushels of cobbed corn shucked by steel-sheathed hands in the cold winter months filling waiting wagons. Theirs are hands that have known the strain of helping new born calves. Their hands kept taut the reins of lunging workhorses in the long rows of cornfields. Their hands pulled weeds from a garden overflowing with fresh vegetables eventually stored and used to very tastefully grace the tables at East View. These hands also caressed the new soft skin of babies, picked mayflowers each spring in the cemetery, and shook readily the other hands of old and new friends.

The dreams of this agrarian philosopher lay in his land and in his children. His vision is not of gold, silver, and material things but an investment of time in the things that will live after him. Boompa was a part of the soil he worked, the rain that nourished his plants, the sunshine that enacted the growing world, and the snow that blanketed the bleakness of winter. The dreams of Boompa lay in his most treasured dream, the part of him and Mom and was most important, his family. He helped us set high goals and never once wavered in his confidence in us that we could achieve anything we set forth to do.

Boompa was a sower and a reaper, a caretaker and a master, a servant and a king. He knew always the meaning of the principles of loving, of truth, trustworthiness, independence, fairness and dependability. Boompa's advice was sound, tempered by a lifetime of trial and error, a lifetime rich with joys and sorrow. All are a compliment to his life lived fully.

Boompa was not a skilled artisan or a professionally educated man. He was never given that opportunity. He was a man of God's earth and God's people. His life was full and rich. It brimmed over into the people he touched. Boompa's love will live on through his legacy of life.

This was written on a cold, snowy night at Carl and Gayle's kitchen table, on East View Farm the eve before Dad's funeral. I had gone to sleep and then awoke, and could not go back to sleep with these words tumbling around in my brain. These thoughts came in complete array and I have not changed them except to clarify and avoid repetition.

Remembrances - Mom

Mor-Mor's name reflects her Scandinavian heritage. Mor is mother in Swedish and Mor-Mor simply implies by name, mother's mother. So it was a natural to call Mom Mor-Mor when Charlotte's children surrounded her and so it came to be. To me she was simply, Mom.

Mor-Mor was not that tall or big a person but she could easily be compared to an oak tree.......not a giant burr oak but perhaps a pin oak. Oaks strong trunks never waver under the strongest of gales. This so describes Mom. Gentle breezes make oak leaves quiver and shudder. Little things affect it. So it was with Mom. The stalwart oak trunk with its vast roots weather many a storm and when finally the turbulence is so intense the trunk breaks and the tree dies, the roots that have grown ever so strongly into the ground remain strong, deep, and unscathed. So it was for Mom. Little daily irritations could disturb her but the bigger problems were always faced undaunted with quiet courage.

Even to the end, Mom was mother and example of a woman of strong will, faith and conviction. Things were always done with decorum by Mor-Mor, she had a quiet flair for what is right and proper and always took pride in a life of quiet dignity. Even during her last night in the hospital, Mom offered a chocolate to one of her nurses helping her. It was the little things that put together made the difference. Things were right or wrong. There was a set of standards that did not waver:

- Bread goes first around the dinner table followed by meat, potatoes, and the rest of the menu.

- Dresses and heels are always worn when shopping downtown in Sioux City. The purse tucked under the arm kept it safe. A glove holder was attached to the purse to clip gloves so they wouldn't get lost.

- Sunday dinners after church are served in the dining room with a centerpiece, linens, and meal complete with a prepared dessert. Holiday meals brought out the best of the linens, sterling silver and food.

- Everyone sits down together for supper.

- Each day of the week has important work to be completed.

- Cleanliness was imperative. Even during the her last night in the hospital Mom asked to have her nails filed. Now the nails on her working hands were always very short and not professionally manicured, but even in her last hours it was important to be prepared.

- Never white until Memorial Day, but never after Labor Day.

Mom's small strong hands were used to doing the many activities of a farm wife and mother. The nervous habit she had of biting her nails left her finger tips cropped. Her hands were wrinkled from all the duties they completed each day in the house and outside during her lifetime. Mom's hands were ready to serve. She was always the lady behind the scenes, never one in front unless it was to pour coffee at some wedding reception. She would be willing to help in the kitchen but never be one to stand out from others leading groups from the front. She did not even enjoy Bible studies in her women's circle groups at church for this reason. She would rather listen than share ideas in front of others. Now don't get the wrong idea. Mom would not ever be thwarted in expressing a view she thought important! She was very strong in her opinions and would address them to appropriate people and express them when she felt it was suitable. She was very articulate and because she was a good listener, when she spoke an idea, question, or comment out loud it was always worthwhile to listen.

Mom enjoyed food! Planning food, gathering recipes for new dishes, growing food, buying food, preserving food, preparing food, serving food, and sharing food were all highly valued activities for mom. Always, some place in the kitchen or pantry, there was a banana, chocolate, hot milk, spice or some kind of cake, or toll-house cookies, or tall, tender dinner rolls, or some golden crisp rusks or a rich Swedish braided coffee-cake could be found on her wooden counter or white metal table. Sometimes it all was hidden from her six, small, snooping hands which were always ready to scoop up and snack on her baked treasures.

Mom always had recipes. She had notebooks and boxes (flat cardboard boxes full of clipped recipes and a large green metal file of carefully gathered recipes from friends and relatives). She had shelves of cookbooks which she delighted in studying. She enjoyed going to food school events at the auditorium in Sioux City. She listened to Kitchen Klatter ladies everyday talk about food and the flavorings they sold in local grocery stores. Their monthly magazine and radio shows each day were visits Mom had with fellow gourmets. When cooking shows began to appear on TV, Mom became an instant fan.

Mom enjoyed the company of her TV in her later years. Even early on in the TV's dawning era she was one of Groucho Marx's most fervent admirers with his program "You Bet Your Life" with the silly duck who would come down and give his guests money if they said the secret word. She loved wrestling matches and was very involved in the pairups which always pitted the good guys against the bad of course. Vern Gagne was her favorite! She enjoyed Art Linkletter's House Party in the afternoon after lunch and the program Queen for a Day later on in the day. Jeopardy and Oprah were other regular programs when she lived on Court Street in the city. The news was another important strand to Mom's days. She became a regular watching the C–Span Senate proceedings and hearings and even local school board arguments and city council proceedings. You could count on Mom knowing what was going on. And, of course, Larry King brought conversation to her living room each evening. One day she explained to me that it was easier to bring her food into her dining room when she was alone and eat with the TV on so she had company eating.

Mom kept up with the local and world's happenings with the newspaper as well as the TV. She was an avid daily reader and could be depended on to know what was going on in the world and in Washington as well as Sioux City. No one was better at the daily crosswords than Mom. Her vocabulary was large and her spelling was excellent. She was not easily stumped by the tricky clues.

Mom was a bulwark of positive faith. I remember a parting reassurance she gave me one morning as I was flying out the back door for the bus

An algebra test faced me this particular day and I was very anxious. Her calm reassurance restored my confidence. "Just do your best.", she said, "And everything will be come out all right." I think this was her motto in all. DO YOUR BEST! Be your best! I remember talking to her when my children were growing up and we were talking one day about John Michael's difficulties in school. "Don't worry!", she said, "Everything will be ok. He will be fine." And she was correct, of course.

The last weekend Mom was in the hospital she was visited by her pastor one afternoon. All of us in her family happened to be there also...... even Uncle Leonard, Aunt Hilda, and Aunt Anna. Pastor read the verses in the Bible where Jesus tries to explain to the disciples his mission to prepare a place for us to go when our time on earth is finished. "My father's house has many rooms." Jesus said, "And I go there to prepare a place for you." Mom with all assurance said quietly, "I know."

Mom, the city woman, had interesting experiences in her profession as a clerk with the Federal Court System in northern Iowa for many years before her marriage. She travelled to Fort Dodge, Waterloo and Dubuque besides sessions in Sioux City. She prided herself in remembering details. She collected fines and kept track of many accounts of bootleggers and other gangsters who came to her with bond money and court related costs. She loved telling of her adventure handcuffed to a prisoner she took from Iowa to Washington D.C. on the train. Pictures of Mom always show a very well dressed fashion plate of her day. She was one of the original "career women".

With all her cosmopolitan experiences she still adapted herself well to the rural setting she found herself in when she married. She and Dad had a special relationship. I remember Dad teasing her, patting her behind when she cooked and stirred at the stove, She popped back a "Don't touch me!" with a little shake for our benefit but the small smile as she turned to him related the message of quiet satisfaction of being touched. She maneuvered the complex work of the farm, raising three children, adapting to a multi-adult home with the care of aging in-laws and Aunt Ruth's presence as a helper with the farm work. Then in their retirement Mom and Dad moved back into Sioux City, just blocks from where she was raised. City woman to country woman back to city woman, all in one lifetime, Mom navigated her life changes with style and found fulfillment wherever she was. She made the best of whatever came her way much like the oak tree with a strong presence, resilient and sturdy even in the strong winds of life.

Remembrances - Aunt Ruth

Sometimes, looking backward over my shoulder has provided a better and more fuller understanding for me of what was happening at the time I was growing up than when I was proceeding forward. For me, this was true especially when I remember my Aunt Ruth. In the midst of the multi-adult family which lived at East View was my Dad's sister, Aunt Ruth, along with Grandpa and Grandma Palmquist, Mom and Dad and three growing children. All eight of us sat around our supper table each night.

Aunt Ruth's presence was part of her devotion for a large portion of her whole life to caring for her parents and to work on the farm. It was Aunt Ruth who perched a pith helmet on her head, put on a long sleeved light blue chambray cotton shirt to cover her arms and spent many days in the fields of East View disking, dragging, plowing, and raking hay. She was the operator of the Booster Buck which lifted the alfalfa to Dad while he arranged the fat, rich, leafy green plant material into tall, rounded stacks. Besides the field work Aunt Ruth also helped with the cows and milking.

She and her brother worked side by side. They had worked together farming from a young age making Grandpa's dream of land ownership a reality. Early letters between Aunt Ruth and her older brother Uncle Wibs at Augustana College in Rock Island, Illinois, record Dad working full time on the Olson farm from the age of 14 and Ruth at 17. One letter records Dad's planting of all the corn on the farm by the age of 16.

Aunt Ruth shared her bedroom with her step-mother Grandma Betty after Grandpa Palmquist died. I remember the bedroom sets purchased the following summer, one for Mom and Dad and one for Ruth. Then Aunt Ruth shared her bed with me. She had a new special spread which she insisted must be folded evenly in half, again into fourths, and lastly cast over the edge of the bottom of the bed each night. Her demands were not happy ones for a six year old putting herself to bed. But, it was one of the things I learned from Aunt Ruth; the importance of order. "Everything should have a place," she used to explain. "When I need scissors, I don't want to look for them. So, if I put them always in the same spot I will know where they are." The importance of taking care of things was always a priority for Aunt Ruth.

Aunt Ruth was a worrier. She was always concerned about people, events, traveling, cooking, or any mundane assortment of everything. Even when we would be driving and let her off at her home, she would always say, "Call me when you get home so I know you get there alright." Now our arrivals and departures were generally too numerous to mention, but when Aunt Ruth knew about them she needed closure.

Worrying about appearances led Aunt Ruth to an almost Victorian, excessively modest attention to details. In the 50's there was a thin voile fabric dress fabric, usually in a light pastel floral which was popular. I remember Mom and Aunt Ruth both had at least one they wore to church. To make sure no one could see through her skirt in the sunlight, Aunt Ruth added a cotton half-slip over her usual white lacy, nylon full slip. Now this was before air-conditioning too.

Appearances apparently important, Aunt Ruth had a pair of the most sensational shoes of all time in the 50's. At least I always thought so anyway. They were black, had many straps even one up around her ankles, and were very highheeled. Always with a hat from her collection perched on her head, Aunt Ruth enjoyed lunches out with friends and going to church.

When I was in high school, Aunt Ruth accepted a position as a house-mother and left East View Farm. She enjoyed working with all the young nurses at the Lutheran Hospital School for Nursing. When she retired, Aunt Ruth moved to her original childhood home at 1610 Court Street in Sioux City.

Aunt Ruth's favorite kitchen activity was baking in her Court Street home. She loved to make coffee-cakes, cakes, desserts, cookies, and lemon meringue rice pudding. It was a different story when it came to cooking. It was not her choice of activity in the kitchen except for necessity. And, as it was her tendency, she worried about every meal she prepared for company. They were delicious affairs alright, but for Aunt Ruth, never good enough.

Always interested in any crafty projects, Aunt Ruth excelled at knitting and crocheting. Her only pre-requisite of our requests was the demand that we use and not just set away her endeavors. Baby blankets, socks, booties were showered on babies. Aunt Ruth's crocheted doilies and finished edges on pillow slips were gorgeous. Some edges of her pineapple patterned doilies were so full they could be starched to ruffle at least two inches high around the edges. Ask for an Icelandic sweater. No problem! Ask for a cream afghan with counted cross stitched roses on top of the yarns. No problem! All treasures for sure.

In Aunt Ruth's retired years she spent several weeks visiting in Illinois. She enjoyed helping with the many tasks of raising young families. She especially enjoyed working with the wash; hanging clothing on outside lines, folding garments from the dryer and pressing out wrinkles.

She always relished the chatter and eating together. I remember especially one New Year's Eve when Char, Bill, Carl and I talked almost all night. Aunt Ruth didn't even nod or blink. Her knitting needles just continued to click and clack. The conversation expanded into talk of the Milky Way Galaxy and near-by galaxies. She was aghast at the thought of the age of sunlight finally falling on her face after travelling through space at the speed of light. Her world was never the same. The crazier the topic, the faster her needles worked.

Another specialty of Aunt Ruth from her retired years was ceramics. She enjoyed taking lessons every week and produced a large number of pieces. Examples she gave away were bunnies and ducks for Easter, small frosted white trees with tiny lights and large poinsettia plates for serving at Christmas time as well as everyday useful items like baking potato shapes for sour cream or lion pencil holders. Aunt Ruth was always busy with something.

Aunt Ruth never married. "She had her chances." Dad once said. But she never chose to leave what she considered her responsibilities. She often said to me in my single professional days until I was married at 31. "Don't end up alone like me, Betty." Someone certainly missed a great lady who would have treated her husband with much love, devotion, and attention to household duties.

Not a formally trained psychologist but a skilled personality former, Aunt Ruth used behavioral techniques she learned somewhere to help me lose a sad, "Wait for me!" approach to life. Sandwiched between a strong, always taller, older and extremely capable daughter and a beloved younger son; as an in between, my chubby short legs and frizzy hair could not compete. My often shed tears must have gotten to Aunt Ruth and she used a Skinner and Pavlov model to change my outlook. Somewhere she must have read about good old positive reinforcement.

Aunt Ruth and I had a round mirror on the west wall of our walk-in closet. She set up a reward system for me of putting up a metallic star every day I would not cry. If the mirror had been a clockface, we started up the bottom from the six and by the time we got to the ten with tightly spaced colorful stars, they were no longer needed. I don't know if it was the extra attention or just the Hawthorne effect of simply knowing someone cared enough for me to expect joy. It worked. The famous divided blue plate Aunt Ruth purchased in Chicago on one of her trips there is a relic of those earlier troubled days.

Aunt Ruth was Aunt Ruth to many, even those outside of our family. She was a people person and friend to all. She never passed judgment or said a bad word about anyone. She always looked for the good. One day she took this tendency a little too far when Char had made a cake in which her young toddler son, Brad with some very "helpful" hands, had substituted salt for the sugar in the recipe. When Aunt Ruth tasted her piece she insisted that it was good, but finally had to admit that it had to be thrown away. It was hard for her to criticize.

Aunt Ruth found it difficult to admit any imperfections in her whole family. She never had a harsh word for anyone. She found good in everyone. She was one of those people who walked with others in life doing her best with what she had. Her love was unending. She was always proud of the accomplishments of all as if they were her own, especially her extended family.

Aunt Ruth left a mark on all of us who grew up in her shadow. As I look back now I realize her silhouette has been ever present, long and strong, full and rich on our lives. If she had known the importance of her life, I am sure she would have been worried if it was good enough.

Remembrances - Grandma Betty

Upstairs in a northwest bedroom of our white wooden Iowa farm home, my Grandma Betty used to sit in a soft, dark brown, velvet-like armed chair. You could often find her reading articles from her life time subscription to Readers Digest.

I don't have many memories of Grandma Betty except for her daily chore of peeling potatoes. I remember sneaking some small cuttings of the newly peeled potatoes from the waiting pan. She would shoo us away telling us it would make our tummies hurt. We still liked to get a piece to crunch. She was always helping some way in the kitchen doing the dishes and such, especially by making pies. But one afternoon, a particular memory with her is stored away in my being as clear as when it happened. So ordinary, but oh so special.

Grandma Betty always wore her graying, brown hair in a small bun at the back of her head. She often wore a small pin with several brown tiger-eye stones across the v-neckline of the simple printed dresses she wore. I remember her sitting one afternoon, mending the heel of a worn sock. Inside the sock she placed a shiny black rounded wooden drumstick shaped tool that stretched the sock heel cloth so Grandma Betty could weave new fabric where there once was a hole.

First, she wove back and forth in long even stitches the length of the opening with her soft mending threads. Next, her needle began its countless crosswise trips over and under the first strands so very closely, the threads formed a solid yarn covering. The warp and weft of the darning threads were woven so carefully the hole eventually would disappear. The like new sock was so perfectly woven it never formed blisters on the heel. From reading Uncle Wibs letters in the early 1900's from Augustana College to the farm, I learned of her extraordinary skills as Uncle Wibs sent his suits back to the farm to fix worn out fabric.

On this particular afternoon, I remember above Grandma's work, a metal frame held a small tan floor lamp with a dark beige silk shade. As the sun went down in the west window, Grandma turned on the lamp to see her work more clearly. My Aunt Ruth who cared for her plants faithfully had guided a prolific green leaved philodendron to trail all around this window. African violets bloomed profusely on a small table near the north window. Nearby was the bed where both Aunt Ruth and Grandma slept each night.

As the sock was almost mended, the sunset glowed into the room, bathing it in golden rays. I sat on a low wooden stool near Grandma's feet, listening to her needle stitching back and forth, watching her patient soft eyes silently moving her small proficient hands, mending oh so carefully. In the dusky sundown silence, love and peace certainly circled this room.

After Words

In northwest Iowa Woodbury County, on top of a hill on the half mile line of the north side of section 23 overlooking the Big Whiskey Creek and the farm fields below known as 'Swede Valley', lays a cemetery dating back to an old Swedish Lutheran church on a plot which was located there before it was destroyed by lightening long ago.

Old worn stones tell us that this is the place where local farmers and their wives have gone when they have no more chores to do, no crops to tend, no berries to put up in mason jars, and no children to mind. Those here no longer fret about wet springs or dry summers, and family disputes. Arguments about fence lines are finally put in proper perspective. Here it is quiet and peaceful on a square of ancient prairie with only the sounds of the leaves of the tall cottonwood trees stirring and rustling in the nearby orchard of East View Farm.

Here a short walk around reveals whole family trees shadowed in lilac bordered plots. Carved in stone, names inscribed tell the story of families from long ago. Blocks of stone are fitting tokens for the names engraved there. Like these stones these people also weathered dry years, wet years, winter storms, and early frosts and stoically thrived none the less. They too stood with their feet firmly planted on the prairie soil and endured the good and the bad that permeates a life.

Here mayflowers stretch their new slender stems each spring through the thatch of big bluestem, Indian grass and side oats gamma grasses. The tulip shaped lavender harbingers of spring shyly present blooms early with the new warm sun each spring. Here the coneflowers and other wild flowers all wave in the breezes of the hot summer sun much as they probably have done on this site for the past few centuries.

Here occasionally a car passing by on the gravel road raises an enormous cloud of dust. A group of birds perch and commune on the telephone wires outside the gate. A hawk circles in skies above while tractors patrol the fields below. The circle of life continues unmindful of our concerns and I'm drawn back once again to this patch of green. Some think heartland defines a location within the land; actually it is the location of the land within the people. How can man create entertainment that competes with the awesome spectacle of a Midwestern thunderstorm? Expensive cologne is less pleasing than the fragrance of newly mown hay. Creations of four star restaurants cannot compete with a sun ripened tomato fresh from the vine or a ruby red strawberry newly picked from the garden or even sweeter from the wild.

And so, dear reader, I leave you with my memories, as real today as when they originally occurred and always a part of who I am no matter where I have lived. Life's rich fabrics of experiences frame who we are and the choices we make. On the wall of my family room is the saying, "Tomorrow's blessings are in the seeds of yesterday". May we be wise enough to notice the world around us each day. In it are the beginnings of new tomorrows.